TAMING
WALL STREET

Stephen Gardner

Taming Wall Street
2018

"A FOOL THINKS HIMSELF TO BE WISE,
BUT A WISE MAN KNOWS HIMSELF
TO BE A FOOL."
- WILLIAM SHAKESPEARE

"THOSE WHO ARE AFRAID OF NEW IDEAS
ARE DOOMED BEFORE THEY EVEN START."
-NAPOLEAN HILL

Preface

I started in the insurance and finance business in 2003. I was still attending college and had been accepted to the David Eccles School of Business at the University of Utah. Upon graduating, I thought I knew a thing or two about money.

I had taken advanced finance courses. I had worked with hedge fund managers one on one. I had grown a successful investment portfolio. Then I entered the 'school of hard knocks' where I've been knocked around more times than I'd like to admit.

Some of my life experience has knocked me down so hard, I didn't know if I could get up. Did I even want to get back up? But I did. I always will. Each knock down has led me to new knowledge.

The stock market has taught me that Wall Street is a wild animal. They know this, but only remind you of it after you've lost money. They remind you that you knew the risk you were taking when you signed up. They even use wild animals to describe themselves. When times are good, they are a stampeding Bull that nothing can stop. When times are bad, they are a ferocious Bear that can rip you and your future to shreds.

Even still, I am not a Wall Street hater. I've just learned a better way to get the upside of Wall Street and avoid the damaging downside. I rejoice when the market is good and I breathe a sigh of relief when the market is bad. The strategies in this book don't lose money. That's right, they are contractually protected against losses.

In 2008 as my 401k was dropping by 38% (I know many that lost more than that) a friend of mine invited me to a private event to learn more about the financial world we worked in but from a totally different way of thinking.

I didn't want to go. It cost $100 and then you had to buy a $25 book and lose 2 days of work. Truthfully, I wanted to believe I knew better. However, I decided to attend and be open to learning something new.

That two day meeting changed the course of my life. Much of the material I share in this book mirrors what I learned then coupled with over a decade of real life experience for myself and many, many clients across the country.

I left that event and told my wife I was planning to quit my job and share this new strategy with everyone I could. Although she thought I was nuts, she supported me and I did just what I said I would. Now 10 years later, I've put my best information into this book.

This book will mostly deal with the strategy I use as my main method of saving and investing. I'll show you how to never lose money again, legally avoid taxes, grow your money every year and have liquid access to utilize your own money to recover the money you typically lose on major purchases. This paragraph and book make some bold statements, but they are true and I stand behind them.

The second strategy is only one short chapter because it is simple and easy to understand. You don't' **EVER** lose money while still getting good returns from old 401k's, IRA's or Roth money. It's a truly amazing way to grow a lump sum of money!

This book will attempt to share several cases of real life uses and examples from my pool of clients. I'm grateful they've allowed me to share their stories alongside my own.

This book will show you how to tame Wall Street and use this incredible money system to your advantage without getting hurt. Wall Street is raging river and I'll show you how to plumb an irrigation canal off her so you can use her momentum to benefit you and your future without all the volatility and stress.

There is a better way in my opinion and this book will show you.

STEPHEN GARDNER

1. FINDING YOUR BEST FUTURE

Recently my wife and I traveled with our three children to Nevada to visit an investment partner and also take a small family vacation. While my wife was off shopping I took my kids over to a private park to play. The park was fenced in, shaded and full of little houses with slides, swings, a splash pad and a maze made out of hedges. The air was filled with laughter and screams. I knew the kids would love it.

After playing for a while, my youngest wanted to enter the maze and see if she could find her way out. The maze had 3 entrances and 3 exits. The hedge was just shy of 4 feet tall. As I stood at the entrance, I noticed that I could follow the path with my eyes from the beginning until the exit. It was full of twists and turns, switchbacks and many promising paths that led to dead ends.

Seeing the end from the beginning allowed me to enter the maze with confidence. My daughter however is young and short. She entered with enthusiasm but had no clue how to reach the exit. All she could see was the hedge towering above her head and what lay directly in front of her feet. I was in no rush so the curious side of me watched to see how this would play out. I occasionally gave her some clues as she progressed through the maze, but for the most part let her find her own way.

Many times she would confidently rush forward on a path and take the corner only to find it led to a dead end. Other times, she would come back from a dead end only to back track on the progress she had already made. She was getting visibly frustrated. At one point I could tell she was feeling lost. I lifted her above the hedge and showed her where we needed to head in order to exit and complete the maze. Even with that, I had to use my higher vantage point to guide her through her journey to the exit.

She eventually completed all 3 routes and was very proud of herself. I, on the other hand, was grateful to be able to see the end from the beginning. Yes, I had to still be patient as I walked through the maze, but I could avoid the dead ends, turn arounds and confusion. I knew where I would end up before I even began.

The next strategy I want to share with you is one I have personally used for many years. I like it so much I actually own multiple plans. It is a strategy I remember feeling confident in, because I could see where it would end up by retirement. I shared the above story about my daughter making her way through the maze because I meet with a lot of people trying to make it through the money maze. I want to help lift you up so you can see the end from the beginning. How many people these days have a fairly good idea on the amount of money they will have by the time they retire?

Maybe you have been saving and investing for a long time and you've experienced investing the way my daughter experienced these mazes. One step forward and two steps back. Confidence when things soared and deep setbacks as the markets dropped or crashed. Almost everyone I've met with who has placed money in the stock market has encountered frustrating dead ends or backtracked on their progress.

Or maybe you are younger or just getting started. You want to avoid the stories you've heard from parents, co-workers, fellow church goers or siblings about what it feels like to lose money. How confident and determined to save would you be, if you could confidently place money and have a good idea of the end result?

This is the high level of confidence you can experience by placing money in a properly built insurance contract that is backed by a company with over 100 years of experience.

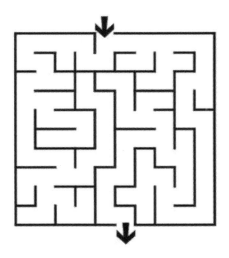

Safety

In his 2017 letter to investors of Berkshire Hathaway, Warren Buffett warned that the markets would drop by 50% in the future. What he couldn't tell his investors was when. Part of Buffett's likeability comes from his humility. He knows he can't control the markets or predict their future so he does his best to accept that there will be losses.

In fact, Berkshire Hathaway has experienced many large drops with many little dips in between. From March 1973 through January 1975, Berkshire stock dropped by 59.1%. In October of 1987 it dropped by 37.1%. From June 1998 to March 2000 it dropped by 48.9% and from September 2008 to March 2009 it dropped by 50.7%.

Do you realize what would happen if you could avoid market loss or negative years?

The insurance contracts we use to protect against downside losses and taxes have been shielding American's money for over 100 years. In fact, one of the companies I utilize has been in business for over 170 years. There aren't many businesses today that have been successfully operating this long. This longevity speaks volumes.

One of my favorite authors wrote about the safety and performance of these contracts. He simply stated, don't lose money ever. Period! What a simple yet profoundly revealing message. I've personally lived through downturns, investments going wrong or companies filing bankruptcy and taking my placement with them. However, I have never lost money in one of my insurance contracts.

We all want to exit the rat race of working one day. You can speed that up when you stop losing money. Stop wasting time waiting several years for a major stock market drop to come back to break even. After the great recession, most people lost close to 50% of their money. It took the S&P 500 five and a half years to get back to breakeven. After the Great Depression, the stock market took 22 years to reach breakeven again. Ouch!

I remember as a child seeing a Warner Brothers cartoon where the main character was climbing a set of stairs only to have the stairs slam shut and resemble a slide. He then slid all the way back to the bottom of the stairs. As a child it was hilarious. As an adult with money on the line, you don't want to experience progress with your retirement money and then suddenly slide backwards in account values because of a market drop. You also don't want to waste time climbing back to where your account value had already been.

Even though I specifically design each of these contracts to be a tax-free vehicle that doesn't lose to the market and provides access to funds before age 59 ½, they are still a life insurance contract. Everyone on the planet has a 100% chance of dying one day. These contracts create a large nest egg of tax-free money for your family upon your death; more than any other investment or savings program. If you know you are going to die and leave your family money, then this is the smartest way to do it.

They say there are only two guarantees in life - death and taxes. This strategy allows you to beat both and have additional living benefits as well.

Over 13 years ago, the first person I ever discussed life insurance with and helped set up a plan, died three months after purchasing his plan. He was in great health and was given the highest health rating from the insurance company. However, no one can predict when someone will pass. I still remember his wife's thank you letter, expressing her gratitude for the money she and her children received. The husband didn't buy his contract with intentions to use it anytime soon, but his family was grateful it was in place.

The greatest risk to your family's financial future is premature death. The beauty of these plans is that when you die, your contract immediately creates a leveraged lump sum of tax-free money for your family. In the event that you live, you will have built a large lump sum of tax-free money you can use in retirement until you eventually die.

You have a 100% chance of dying one day and a 100% desire to retire from work one day. This strategy kills two birds with one stone and makes it stress-free along the way.

2. CONFIDENCE TO SAVE

One of my insurance contract clients of many years admitted to me recently in our annual review that this is her favorite savings program. She also shared with me that before owning a contract she wasn't saving enough money. She never felt confident in the products she used for saving. With her insurance contract, she knew it would earn more than the bank. And she felt confident that she could legally avoid unnecessary taxes eating into her growth. Best of all, her plan gave her great comfort in knowing she wouldn't wake up in retirement and find 50% of her money had disappeared like her father experienced in 2008.

Maybe you have had these same thoughts. Here are some actual comments I have heard on such a regular basis I have them memorized. "I don't save enough because the bank only pays .1%". "I'm not saving much because I think the market is going to crash and take my money." "Nothing pays very much interest unless you are willing to take lots of risk." "What the stock market gives, it eventually takes away. I just end up with the money I put in or less." "Sometimes I feel like I am building my stock broker and Uncle Sam's retirement, but not my own."

The truth is we all need to save more money consistently year in and year out. That being said, I understand people's worries about losing money to the market or inflation due to low interest rates. I had these same thoughts myself until I adopted the insurance contract strategy.

Would you save more if you knew you would receive a good rate of return? Would you save more if you weren't worried about losing your money or interest gained each year? Think you would save more if you knew that your money wouldn't be taxed in the future? I believe most people would. They simply need a program that is solid and breeds confidence.

Nowadays people want high returns while making low contributions. Unfortunately, a large percentage of Americans either don't have a system, aren't saving enough money or don't have the right incentive to save money for the future.

46% of Americans die with less than $10,000 in savings according to the National Bureau of Economic Research.

40% of US workers feel they need $1 million to retire, yet 30% of baby boomers preparing to retire or already in retirement have less than $50,000. That's a $950,000 shortfall. This less than adequate retirement nest egg either came from not saving enough or losses.

The insurance contracts we utilize allow clients to focus on a savings system. This one system may be the only savings vehicle you will need. I will recommend others but it is that good. It allows you to focus on your career, because you don't have to track the markets each day. It allows you see over the maze hedge so you can see the end from the beginning. It allows you to plug into 100+ year old companies that handle everything for you from start to finish. Having all this in place saves you time, energy and money. Best of all, it will help you attain your goals without having to stress at every turn. Most people dream of a stress-free retirement but imagine also having a stress-free journey while saving for retirement.

Keep in mind, that the groups I work with all operated during the Great Depression while still protecting and increasing client's money. Imagine a contract that kept money safe and grew while the rest of the country and banks were failing. These companies have survived every major financial up and down that America has thrown at them. In fact, one has been in business since before the Civil War.

I'll repeat what was said earlier about these contracts; never lose money to the market, period!

When it comes to money, most people tend to only see two worlds for growing their money. One world is Wall Street and the other world is the bank. Each world has a different marketing message and philosophy on money.

An observation I've had after working with thousands of people over the years, is that we put a lot of pressure on Wall Street and Banks and not nearly enough on ourselves. We've become interest rate chasers and not dedicated savers. I think saving is more imperative. Most people are not master investors and won't hit critical mass on earning more than they can save for a long time.

The more you save, the more you'll have.

So many times I see clients get hung up on rate of return. Yet most people fail to realize that what they contribute to their future can build their wealth faster than what their money can earn. This is why people get sucked into Wall Street when interest rates at the bank are low.

For example, if you earn $50,000 per year and save 10%, that is $5000 saved per year. The next year, your $5000 may earn 5% and add $250 of interest to your account, but you can add another

$5000 to the account by being a dedicated saver. That is 20x what your money earned for you in interest. I'm not saying don't put your money to work. You absolutely should, but what you save will be higher than what your money can earn for many years.

To match the $5000 you can save per year, you would need to have $100,000 earning 5% to equal your contribution amount. At $5000 a year earning 5% annual, it will take you 14 years to have $100,000. So eventually, your interest earnings will catch up with the amount you are able to save, but this only happens if you are first a good saver. Saving regularly is the first step.

"A Portion Of All You Earn Is Yours To Keep."

-Richest Man in Babylon

Again, what you save matters most for most of your life. I meet with so many people that don't want to save like they know they should so the conversation inevitably turns to how can they earn 10% or 20% or 100% return on their money. I'm not saying this is impossible but you need money to go make money. Of course you could use other people's money but you still have to cut them in on the deal and you have to have an incredible track record of handling and growing money or no one will lend you money.

I once read a tale of two friends. One friend saved $5000 a year and was able to consistently earn 10% annual year in and year out. The other was a good saver and saved $10,000 a year but was only able to earn 5% annual year in and year out. The story then ends by saying the friend that earns 10% interest won't catch up to the friend that earns 5% for 24 years. See images below to see the math at work.

< Home **Compound Inte...** Advanced

Principal Amount	**0**
Monthly Deposit	**416.5**
Period (month)	**288**
Annual Interest Rate%	**10**

Compounding   **Annually**

Reset	Calculate

Total Principal: **119,952.00**
Interest Amount: **345,967.25**
Maturity Value: **465,919.27**
APY: **10.0000%**

Email	Interest Table

$5000 per year at 10% compounded interest.

‹ Home **Compound Inte...** Advanced

Principal Amount | 0

Monthly Deposit | 833

Period (month) | 288

Annual Interest Rate% | 5

Compounding   **Annually**

| Reset | Calculate |

Total Principal: **239,904.00**
Interest Amount: **216,895.98**
Maturity Value: **456,799.98**
APY: **5.0000%**

| Email | Interest Table |

$10,000 at 5% compounding interest.

So for 24 years the friend earning 10% each year gets to 'brag' about his interest rate and his growth, but the very interest rate he is bragging about won't catch up to his friend who is saving more money each year for 24 years. I don't care what age you are at when you start, 24 years is a long time.

Now let me ask you this, what is more likely, that you could average 10% for 24 years or 5% for 24 years? Obviously, 5% is more realistic. So how is this possible? Because the friend put the pressure on himself to save more and not on the interest rate that he could not control, he maintains the lead on account value increases for 24 years. **Work with the side of the equation that you can control.**

As you improve your skills, move up the company ladder and expand your business or income, you will be able to save a greater amount of money. Eventually the goal is to have your principal passively earning more than you can contribute. As you near retirement, it should be earning more than you could earn working full-time. What you contribute makes a huge difference over time.

I'm not saying interest rate is not important so please don't take that away from this chapter. I'm simply pointing out that we should first have our focus on saving as much as we can consistently. Then, as we have money to work with, we can venture into investments that have the ability to earn higher rates of return.

With a properly structured cash value insurance contract, you can do just this. You can start off saving as much as you can in a program that will earn between 5-6%. As you have money, you could use that money to stop losing interest and depreciation on car purchases, have access to conservative interest rates for buying real estate or you can put that money to work in investments that allow you to put the money back into your plan as you finish with it. Many examples will be given in coming chapters.

Until this time, save as much as you can. What you save matters most and the programs in this book will show you how earn the interest rates you need.

3. HOW IT WORKS!

There are hundreds of insurance carriers in America. There are thousands of different insurance contracts. I only believe in and trust a handful. Very few insurance carriers have the program I am describing or even allow agents to design them the way that best benefits the client.

There are two main strategies for building wealth with this concept. The first is a contract that grows by a conservative rate of return every single year and provides a dividend if the company performs better than expected. The groups I work with have never missed an interest payment, even in bad economies and they have issued a dividend to contract holders every year for over 100 years. The interest is guaranteed. This is the way my ultra conservative clients like to grow their money. Imagine between now and retirement, having growth every single year on your money. Non-stop, uninterrupted compounding interest.

Below is a table that demonstrates 5% growth year in and year out with no losses compared to the actual performance of the S&P 500 from 2000-2017. There is something powerful about just knowing your money will increase every single year regardless of the stock market or the economy.

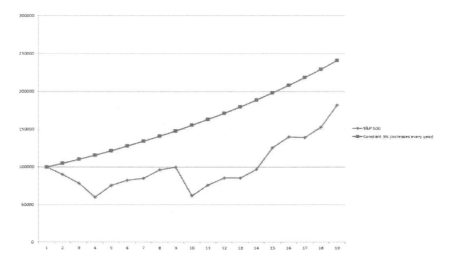

The second strategy for building wealth in these programs involves linking to different stock market indexes without actually placing your money in the stock market. Your contract is credited interest based on how the markets perform. You are also protected against having a negative year when they don't perform or worse, if they drop like we've seen in the past. The insurance company takes on the risk and protects you in two ways.

The first way money is protected by the insurance company is by having what is called a floor. This means your money participates in the upside growth of the stock market but can never go below zero. For example let's say the stock market increases by 8% from the time you place money until your anniversary date, your account would be credited 8%. Let's say the market earned nothing, your account is credit with a 0%. Now let's say the market dropped by 25%, your account is still credited with a 0%. While everyone else is upset and stressed or delaying retirement, you are sitting back on the sidelines with no losses from the stock market. Just search the market returns for the past 100 years and you will see plenty of drops or just consider the major stock market drops previously shared by Warren Buffett. Markets lose and sometimes they lose big. Just because the market loses, doesn't mean you have to participate.

The second way money is protected is also the mechanism that helps with its growth. It is called the annual reset. Each year on the anniversary date of your policy, the insurance company assesses what it owes you for the year based on how the stock market index performed. At the same time, it resets and locks in your principal and gain for the year. For example, let's say you have $100,000 and the market is up 8%. Your money would grow in this example to $108,000 and lock that value in place. You can now never go lower than $108,000 unless you take money out of your account or stop paying on your policy for an extended period of time.

With the annual reset locking in your money and gains each policy year, you see over time your account values rising with an occasional flat year but never a market loss. Compare this to the stock market where you see rising and falling account values each year. Does this strategy always go up? No. I've seen flat years in my own plans. Does it lose to the market? Also a no! This is the way I prefer to grow my money. I'll take several years of ups and a few of flat over the stress of trying to predict whether the markets will be up or down.

Humans also have this fear of missing out on something good. They hear these stories of the few that make it rich with the stock market so they jump on the bandwagon. Then they lose money and because of fear they pull out of the market. They buy high and sell low because of fear of losing and fear of missing out. What if you could eliminate the fear of missing out and the fear of losing? With this concept you can!

Surprise, the returns reported by mutual funds aren't actually earned by investors.
Jack Bogle, founder of Vanguard

Below is a line graph of how an actual indexing plan performed with a zero floor and 12.5% cap compared to the actual performance of the S&P 500 from 2000-2017. The markets can bring incredible growth but as soon as there are losses, the indexing strategy takes off because all it can experience during a down market is a flat year. No more negative years or account values dropping.

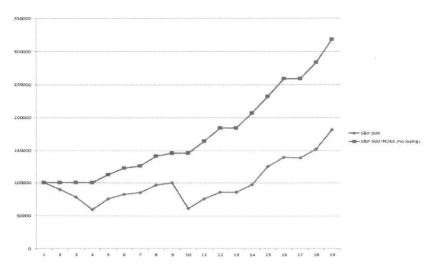

These two ways of growing money give you control and predictability. You can't control the stock market, but you can control the devastation of losses from being directly invested in the stock market. With the first strategy described that grows year in and year out like clockwork, you have a very predictable system. With the strategy that earns based on market index performance, you can use the past to help form your decisions, but you can also see that most decades have more ups than downs and you can use that pattern to your advantage.

Again, the negative years you see in the stock market are represented on a graph as deep plunging lines while in the index strategy you see a flat line indicating no growth and no loss. Both strategies allow you to focus on a system that helps you see the end from the beginning and avoid setbacks.

Insurance companies behave differently with money than Wall Street. Insurance companies think 20-50 years into the future. They plan conservatively and with a long term approach. Wall Street however, displays a pattern of seeking short term gains and the risk of losing money. Their hope is to push gains as high as they can before the next stockholders meeting or before the next quarterly review with a client.

Legally ditch future taxes

A large percentage of my clients own these contracts or multiple contracts just for the sheer fact that they can legally avoid future taxes. Many of these clients are wealthy doctors or business owners, yet all the same advantages apply to people like you and me. No one wants to pay more taxes than they have to. No one!

How would you like a savings account that grows tax-free as it earns, allows for tax-free access to your money and transfers wealth to your family income tax-free?

I want to show you a way to legally avoid tax in the future. The first time I share this information with people, they think it sounds too good to be true, but it is all verifiable and true. These tax advantaged plans are what guru Tony Robbins calls a rich man's Roth IRA. Except unlike a Roth IRA, it doesn't have the income restriction from making too much money. It also doesn't have a contribution restriction for those that want to save more than a couple thousand dollars a year in a tax friendly program. And it doesn't have an age restrictions that dictate when and how you can access your money.

Taxes will be the single biggest factor to separate you from your retirement dreams.

Best-selling author and tax advisor, **Ed Slott**

Imagine you have just started your first day of retirement. Maybe you plan to golf or fish. Maybe you plan to travel or just be a home body, living by your own schedule. Now imagine you were disciplined enough to accumulate $1 million in your retirement account. As you start retirement, do you want that $1 million to be taxable or do you want the $1 million to be tax-free?

I have never met someone who hoped to wake up in retirement with $1 million that is still under obligation to be taxed. Yet a huge percentage of the people I work with are saving most of their money in 401ks and IRAs that will absolutely need to be taxed. People say they don't want taxes during retirement but then they set themselves up for large tax bills right when they depend on the money the most. When we know better, we can plan better.

Will your current plan set you up to have tax-free money or money that still needs to be taxed?

The truth is we hate taxes so much that we try to eliminate them right now. I hear so often from advisors about the importance of diversification but rarely about diversifying a client's future tax burden. Next to a home or major medical expense, taxes are one of the largest expenses we have in life. Isn't it just as important to diversify your future tax burden? Most people I've worked with that are already retired wish they had done better tax planning during their working years. You get to choose your future tax burden by the way you save and invest your money, so choose wisely.

People like 401ks because they are easy to set up and they don't think about pulling money out each month. It's automatic and easy to get accustomed to a smaller pay check. Sometimes you even get an employer match which is free money. However, as this money compounds over the years, so does your future tax obligation and remember, Uncle Sam gets to decide how much he gets from your money, not you.

Another major downside to qualified plans like a 401k or IRA is that you can't access your money until age 59 ½ without paying a penalty and taxes. Wait, it is your money, right!? Is it really to your advantage to lock up your own money for several decades? Most people agree that it isn't to their advantage, but they've bought into the savings plan designed by Wall Street and the Government as the only way to prepare for retirement.

If you aren't involved in the insurance world each day like I am, then you probably didn't hear about the new world record set regarding the highest life insurance policy ever purchased. In 2014, the Guinness Book of World Records announced that a mysterious tech billionaire in California bought a $201 Million life insurance policy. That's $201,000,000 to help it sink in.

Why on earth would a billionaire need $201 million in death benefit? Understanding money and heavy taxation, I can only imagine he wanted to pass as much of his money on tax-free as is legally possible. You don't have to be a billionaire to care about your life's work and life's savings being gobbled up in taxes by Uncle Sam upon your death.

In fact, according to the Wall Street Journal, the top 10% of wealthiest households in America own 55.1% of all the tax-free money inside these private insurance contracts. The bottom 50% of households own 6.5% with the middle and upper class owning the rest. If success leaves clues, the clue the wealthy are leaving is pretty clear - don't lose money and don't pay taxes unnecessarily! In most cases, the wealthy aren't any smarter than the average person, but they are smarter about where they put their money and how they legally avoid taxes.

I want you to stop reading for a minute and ponder this thought: How do you feel every April when you have to file a tax return and pay Uncle Sam more money? How do you feel knowing they decide what money belongs to them and not to you? How do you feel about the government deciding what amount of money they will receive before your children, favorite charity, church or whoever you plan to leave your money to?

With life insurance, it has already been decided and protected by law that Uncle Sam won't get to tax your insurance death benefit. Not being taxed on our money while alive and upon death is a plan we can all live with.

Did you know that America divorced herself from England over 1-2% tax rates? Our founding fathers cut the cord, risked their lives and went to war over 1-2% taxes from England. Yet today we are taxed up to 37% of our income on top of nearly 100 other taxes we pay for the right to live in this country. When it comes to taxes we have become complacent. We've allowed a bloated government to tell us how much they want of our hard earned money. Being smart about taxes could make all the difference in the quality of retirement you get to experience.

The best way to teach your children about taxes is
to eat 30% of their ice cream.
Bill Murray

Life insurance companies have protected American wealth from Uncle Sam for nearly 100 years, but it might not always be that way. Recently, the government and those running for president have threatened to remove the tax-free nature of life insurance. Removing the tax benefits has gone to the Hill several times to be voted on and stayed intact but each year it gets harder. Those who own a contract will be grandfathered in on the tax advantages if the laws are changed in the future.

Is having your money tax-free while it grows, while you use it in retirement and passing it to your children important to you? Then this is a strategy worth researching and looking at the numbers. I'll give some examples in this chapter that will help you see how it grows and can be used. I won't really be able to show the taxes, but then again I don't need to because in a properly built contract, you don't have to worry about taxes.

How to get more out of every dollar

Banking is necessary. Banks are not.
Wells Fargo 2004 Annual Statement

I was fortunate enough to learn about this next strategy from the best-selling author of the Infinite Banking Concept, Nelson Nash. I attended a night time seminar he conducted in Salt Lake City. During one of the breaks I approached Mr. Nash to thank him for what I had learned and possibly get a photo together. I remember he looked me in the eyes and said "you should always be in two businesses; whatever you do for a living and banking. Understanding banking will bless your life."

Now that I have owned these contracts personally for many years and have used the money in them to my advantage, I more fully understand what he was trying to teach me back then. In this section I will show you how to use the cash value in your plan to your advantage. I'll show you how to build a nest egg that you can use for making major purchases like cars, boats, RV's, rental properties, etc. Most people will finance more money through banks for homes, cars and other loans, than they will ever save, so I want to show you how to kill two birds with one stone and come out significantly further ahead than most people.

According to a recent survey by Voya Financial, 45% of Americans admitted they would rather give up financial security before they give up their cars, smart phones or family vacations. Why not learn how to incorporate these wants into your savings plan so you can do what you want and still have what you will need in the future?

One of my favorite aspects of these insurance contracts is the liquid cash value they build and make available to the owner. This is money you can access without age restrictions like a 401k or IRA. This is money you can use for whatever you like. It is money you don't have to show hardship or proof of employment to access. There is no credit check or mountain of paperwork to get through underwriting to qualify. This is simply your money!

In these contracts, a portion of your money goes into a cash account that earns interest while a smaller portion goes to pay for the death benefit costs of the life insurance. When done correctly, you should have cash value from year one. It does take a few years for most people to build up enough cash value to use it for major purchases, but once you have it, you can really use it to your advantage.

It's the only financial product I know of that can earn interest in two places at the same time. When you use the money, you can either take your money out and stop earning interest just like a savings account or you can use the insurance company's money with a conservative interest payment and have your money continue to earn interest as if it were never taken from the policy. This happens because your money isn't used. Your money acts as collateral so it is technically always earning interest in the policy.

Car buying example

There are two types of people in this world;
those that pay interest and those that earn it. Make sure
you are on the earning side of the interest equation.
Dan Kitchen

I want to share some real numbers I put together to help a client of mine purchase a truck from the plan he set up several years earlier. As of writing this, I know clients with a 3.99% car loan and others as high as 24%. The one with 24% really needs this concept but the one with 3.99% would benefit too and you'll see why. We'll be using 7% APR.

The client opened a policy several years ago with a $600 a month savings plan or $7200 a year. After 5 years he had $32,904 in liquid cash and $281,295 in tax-free death benefit if anything happened to him. One morning he called me to ask if I could remind him why it was better to use his insurance contract versus financing his truck through the bank. He let me know he was looking at a $25,000 truck with a 7% interest rate and a 60 month pay off plan.

As we calculated the payment, both our calculators came up with a $495 payment. This was a payment he could afford. I then walked him through an example of using his insurance contract verses a bank. I'll walk you through the same example so you can see the numbers. He was shocked by the final results and ultimately used his own money from his insurance contract to make the purchase.

Imagine two families are at the point where they need to purchase a new car. The first family decides to go to their local bank where their families have been banking for three generations and everyone knows their name. They fill out all the bank paperwork and apply for a loan. The bank checks their credit, verifies their income and checks their employment history. They also do a debt-to-income verification to make sure they are good at repaying past loans and aren't over leveraged with debt. After all is said and done, they are approved for a car loan of $25,000 with a 7% interest rate with a 60 month repayment plan.

The second family has been safely saving money inside their insurance contract and decides to borrow some of the equity to finance the car purchase. They call the life insurance company and request their money be mailed to them. The insurance company verifies they are the owner and sends them the check. There is no credit check or proof of employment. It's your money and they send it to you.

At this time the insurance group will remind you that it is up to you to pay back the loan on your terms and they will leave it up to you to decide how that happens. They also remind you that your borrowed money will continue to earn interest because they will be lending you money from the life insurance company's general fund and will be using your money as collateral. You decide your repayment schedule will look exactly like it would have with the bank, but you will pay it to yourself instead of the neighborhood bank. You will pay $25,000 back over that 60 months with 7% interest.

Option 1: Family 1 Traditional Car financing through a Bank

Auto Loan period:	5 years (60 months)
Monthly payment:	$495
Auto Loan amount paid:	-$25,000
Interest @ 7% paid:	-$4,700
Total paid to BANK:	**-$29,700**
Car value after 5 years:	+$12,000
Total Loss:	**-$17,700**

Most people look at this car buying example and they understand it because it is the way they have always purchased cars up to this point. You buy a car, you pay the bank and at the end of 5 years it isn't worth much. Most have accepted this as the only way to buy a car. Family #1 pays $495 a month for 60 months and after 5 years has paid $29,700 to the bank.

Remove the car for a minute and let's just talk numbers. If a financial adviser said "give me $25,000 and in 5 years I will give you back $12,000, you would run as far away from them as possible. Yet we walk into banks hoping our credit and income are good enough for this exact losing scenario! We beg the bank to rob us. Not any more!

Really quick – up to this point in your life, how many cars have you owned? How many of them did you lose money on or end up upside down in when trying to buy the next car? Keep this in mind while you learn a smarter way to control and use your own money.

According to the American Automobile Association, over 38% of car owners are upside down with their car value.

Let's break this down to better understand what has happened. You bought a $25,000 car and at the end of 5 years have paid $29,700 to the bank. You paid $4,700 to finance the car. Banks don't want you to know what this car purchase is really costing you so they only speak to you in terms of <u>monthly payments</u>. On top of that, they use the acronym APR to disguise how much you will really pay in interest on the car. You think you are paying 7% because this is what you have been led to believe, but you are really paying 18.8%. Take the interest of $4,700 and divided it into the car price of $25,000 you get .188. To calculate the interest rate you multiply it by 100 and you get 18.8% total interest. You paid 18.8% interest on your car purchase! It's no wonder you feel like you aren't accumulating wealth! The bank is the real winner here. You've always been on the losing side of the interest equation. This is why banks are the most lucrative businesses in the world. There is a more productive way to finance cars and other major purchases, but the banks don't want you to know about it. If you knew this information and made purchases this alternative way, you would be a competitor and they need you to be a customer.

When you finance your car through a bank, you end up paying interest for the right to borrow the banks money. You also end up losing value on the car each year because mileage, wear and tear, etc. In this example you lost $4,700 to interest and $13,000 to depreciation for a total loss of $17,700. Interest payments and depreciation can end up costing you tens of thousands of dollars on each car you purchase. Imagine buying this way on 10 vehicles and losing out on $177,000. Ouch!

Again, the traditional way of buying cars through your local bank or credit union may seem incredibly normal to most people because this is what you have been told to do most of your life by the banks. Let me repeat that, **THE BANK** taught you to buy cars this way! They've trained you to make them money.

However, there is a better way to buy cars and you won't look at car buying the same way once you learn this strategy. It's like the first time someone pointed out the arrow between the E and the x in the FedEx logo. It had always been there but I just didn't know it. But now I do notice it and every time I see that arrow, I remember I am buying cars the smarter way. You can, too!

At first glance there doesn't seem to be much difference between family 1 and family 2. The amount borrowed is the same. The interest rate is the same. The monthly payment timeframe is the same. The amount you end up with at the end of the loan is **significantly different!** With traditional financing you are taking money out of your pocket and giving it to the bank. The bank has possession of your money.

By being their own source of financing, family 2 was taking money out of their pocket and sticking it in their other pocket. At the end of 5 years, they've paid themselves $29,700 instead of the bank. There is no fuzzy math here. You had to make the car payment to someone; in this case it was to yourself! So now family 2 has possession of the $29,700 inside their contract. Plus they have a $12,000 car they can sell for a total of $41,700 placed back in their possession for the next purchase. Trust me, this is a good problem to have.

Option 2: Family 2 Car financing through their insurance contract

Auto Loan period:	5 years (60 months)
Monthly payment:	$495
Auto Loan amount paid:	+$25,000
Interest @ 7% paid:	+$4,700
Total paid to YOURSELF:	+$29,700
Car value after 5 years:	+$12,000
Total Gain:	+ $41,700

At the end of 5 years of paying on a car, would you rather have $12,000 or $41,700? It's a no brainer. In fact, it's very lucrative and beneficial for the one receiving the money. From now on that gets to be you! Quit making the banks rich and start making yourself rich by being your own source of financing on a car you would have purchased and driven anyway. As you can see, there was no additional out of pocket expense or payment eating into your monthly cash flow.

What if I told you it actually gets better than this? Remember a few paragraphs ago I mentioned that when you borrow money out of your insurance contract it continues to earn interest as if it were never gone? Let me show you an example of this exact scenario but with the $25,000 continuing to earn 5% each year. Notice I didn't say 10% or some crazy high number? Just 5%!

Year 1- $25,000 has grown to $26,250.

Year 2- $26,250 has grown to $27,562.

Year 3- $27,562 has grown to $28,941.

Year 4- $28,941 has grown to $30,388.

Year 5- $30,388 has grown to $31,907.

Over 5 years the $25,000 in your contract continued to earn interest and grew in value by $6,907. If we add the $6,907 to the $41,700 you put back into your pocket for a total of $48,607. We still had to pay interest so we minus the $4700 for a total increase of $43,907. Remember we pay simple interest to the insurance company so our money can continue earning compounding interest. This is the power that comes from paying yourself like the bank, having your loan amount compound interest each year as if it were never gone and recoup the money you lose to depreciation.

The total economic value added to your family is $43,907 by being your own source of financing. If the math seems fuzzy, please read through it again. In fact, I recommend looking it over a few times to let it really sink in. I assure you there are no tricks or smoke and mirrors going on here. The math doesn't lie. When you take control of your own money and put it to good use, it will grow for you. The money in your contract will continue to earn interest whether it is inside or outside of the plan. By using these idle dollars to your advantage, you can turn ordinary purchases into retirement building dollars. After all, who do you trust more than yourself? This is the power of financing your own purchases with a plan that continues to earn interest even when you access your money.

Take a minute to run the numbers on your personal car loan(s). Take your monthly payment and multiply it by the number of payments you set up for repayment. How much do you stand to lose in interest and depreciation? How many cars will you buy over your lifetime? Do you have children? Will they need cars, too? Just by harnessing the flow of money from car purchases, you can put a significant amount of money back into your pocket where it is safe and available to use on the next purchase or in retirement.

Cash for cars is the worst

One of the worst things you can do with your money is buy a car in cash. It loses value as soon as you drive it off the lot. You give up the right to use that money for other needs or wants and it stops earning interest immediately. Plus a car is a depreciating asset so it loses value over time while the money you used to pay for the car in cash loses future buying power thanks to inflation.

In a perfect world you could use your money and keep it earning interest. This perfect world exists but only in a properly designed permanent life insurance contract. Cash value insurance is the only financial product that allows you to continue to earn interest on your money, even when you have taken it out for buying a car or rental property or flipping real estate or whatever the purchase may be.

The second you withdraw money from the bank or use it to buy a car, it stops earning interest. It's gone! The bank removes it from their ledgers and therefore it stops earning interest.

It's important to understand that you finance everything in this world when you have money. You either pay for the right to use someone else's money or you give up the right to earn interest on your own. This is called opportunity cost and it is a real thing.

Let's say you had the opportunity to buy a piece of real estate with your cousin and she went on to earn 50% on her money when she completed the project and sold the home. That is opportunity cost. You lost out on money you could or should have earned by putting it or keeping it somewhere else.

So what does opportunity cost have to do with buying a car? Well, a lot!

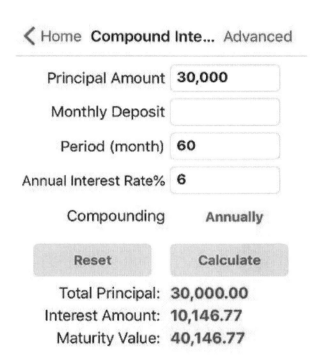

< Home Compound Inte... Advanced

Principal Amount	**30,000**
Monthly Deposit	
Period (month)	**60**
Annual Interest Rate%	**6**
Compounding	**Annually**

Reset	Calculate

Total Principal: **30,000.00**
Interest Amount: **10,146.77**
Maturity Value: **40,146.77**

Let's say you had $30,000 at the bank and you were able to earn 6% interest each year on your money. Leaving your money in this earning environment coupled with compounding interest would have your money growing from $30,000 to $40,146.77. That's $10,146.77 in interest.

By removing your money from this earning environment it earns 0% and compounding interest ceases to exist on this money. Instead you will actually lose the $10,146.77 of opportunity interest and you will lose to the car depreciating in value. After 5 years, the car will most likely be valued at $15,000. You took a 50% loss on your money.

Because money loses value every year its best to buy something today with someone else money and pay it back with a weaker and weaker dollar in the future. You need to keep your money earning. With a traditional loan you will lose less to interest but you will still lose to deprecation so you've improved one area of your finances, but we can do better.

‹ Home **Auto Loan Calculator**

Vehicle Price	**30,000**
Sales Tax (%)	
Max Sales Tax	Note
Fees (taxable)	
Fees (no-tax)	
Down Payment	
Trade-in Value	Note
Amount Owed on Trade-in	
Interest Rate (%)	**6**
Loan Term	**60** months

Reset   Calculate

Monthly Payment: **579.98**
Sales Tax: **0.00**
Amount Financed: **30,000.00**
Total Interest: **4,799.04**

If you financed the car for 60 months or 5 years at 6%, you would pay $4,799.04 in interest. If you left your $30,000 to earn the $10,146.77 you'd still be ahead by $5,347.73.

That's the interest you earned, minus the interest you paid to the bank on the car loan.

$10,146.66 - $4,799.04 = $5,347.73.

Using OPM (Other People's Money) to buy the car and pay it back over time resulted in an extra $5,347 in your pocket. Who couldn't use an extra $5,300 just by understanding finance a little better? But wait, it gets better.

Now imagine you took the time to fund a properly built cash value policy that earns every year. You would have an incredible advantage over most Americans when it comes to buying cars and being smart with your money. With the right plan and company, you can have your cake and eat it, too.

Imagine being able to leave your $30,000 growing, but also use that $30,000 to buy the car you want. This is called making money work in two places. Your money will continue to earn compound interest without the interruptions. You will also be able to pay back the insurance company with a weaker and weaker dollar each year until you've paid off the loan. By paying yourself back this way, most people pay off their car in about 51 months. The remaining 9-10 payments to finish off your 60 month commitment are premium that goes into your plan to increase your wealth.

With one of these plans, your entire payment goes to principal reduction on your loan and interest can be paid or absorbed on your anniversary date. Traditional loans like cars and homes have each payment going toward interest and what's left towards principal. In the case of a mortgage it takes 20 years before more of your money goes to principal and less to interest. This is being smarter with your money.

Then best of all, you take the remaining money from selling your car and dump it into your plan or if you don't have room put it in savings or open a new plan. Whatever route you go, the end result is more money. Would you like more money? Of course you would! This strategy does it for you.

Stop buying cars in cash because you give up interest and control. Stop financing with a bank because you build up their bottom line instead of your own. At the end of the day, don't you want to build your own wealth and not the banks? Now you can and I can show you how it is done. Let me mentor you and help you make more money.

4. WHAT ELSE CAN I FINANCE?

Here are a few ideas to consider:

- **Trucks**
- **Cabin**
- **Church Service Mission**
- **Boats**
- **Luxury Vacation**
- **RV for traveling**
- **Real Estate**
- **Business Opportunities**
- **College**
- **Your Own Mortgage**
- **Equipment to businesses**
- **Rental Properties**

I'm sure you have a list of things you would like to own, experience or do. Once your contract is funded, you can use the money for anything you want. I have clients that have purchased jet skis, gone to Hawaii for a month, landscaped their yard, and paid off student loans and credit card debt. I have people that have pulled money out to buy and flip real estate. People have even purchased cabins and vacation homes once they had accumulated enough money in their plan.

"To become financially independent you must turn part of your income into capital; turn capital into enterprise; turn enterprise into profit; turn profit into investment; and turn investment into financial independence."

-Jim Rohn

Don't throw your money to the wolves on Wall Street! Save your money and then lend it to yourself. Once you become experienced at using your plan, you can start looking into being a source of financing on all your major purchases. This is where you can really fast-track the growth on your money. Whatever business you are in, also stay in the banking business and get your money working for you and not for Wall Street. Be your own source of financing and your own best customer!

Imagine the above scenario of buying your cars through your own insurance contract played out 10 times over the course of your life. Imagine how much further ahead you would be at retirement if you thought and behaved like a bank!

Other popular purchases

I'm not going to be as detailed as I was on the car example because I think you are smart enough to grasp the idea. However, I run across a large number of people that either own or dream of owning an RV or a boat. These are the type of toys that build lasting memories for a family but can also really eat into your wealth when purchased the traditional way.

RV purchase

Let's say you want to buy an RV and you find the one that best accommodates your family for $85,000. Let's assume taxes and fees are built into the final price. As I write this section, a 15 year loan with excellent credit is 5.74%.

RV Loan period:	15 years (180 months)
Monthly payment:	$705
RV Loan amount paid:	-$85,000
Interest @ 5.74% paid:	-$41,970
Total paid to Bank:	**-$126,970**
RV value after 15 years:	+$20,000
Total Loss(interest & Depreciation):	**-$106,970**

Oww! That is a huge price to pay for owning an RV. **Money handed over to the bank is money you will never see or be able to use again.** This truth in lending breakdown makes owning an RV look foolish. Again, we ask ourselves *why am I not further ahead financially?* The point on this example is not to burst your bubble or crush your dreams. It's to point out a hidden truth, but don't worry because there is also a solution. Now imagine these same numbers but you are using your insurance contract and putting the money back into your own pocket. You can have the fun toy and the memory maker without feeling resentful or broke at the end of the day.

The $41,970 in interest is nearly 50% of the price of the RV. Interest charges combined with depreciation is what makes buying depreciating assets a losing battle.

Imagine having the $126,970 back in your insurance contract plus a $20,000 RV you can sell for a total of $146,970 back in your possession. If you plan to own an RV, you are going to live through this scenario. Which outcome do you want to have at the end of the loan?

Ski Boat Purchase

Another toy that can quietly eat away at your wealth is a boat. New ski boats today can range from $50,000 to $150,000. I know many families attribute boating together as some of their favorite memories. There is something about cheering each other on while being dragged behind a boat at 30 mph. I get it! Our family loves boating. There is a way to make a boat purchase work for you.

Let's say you want to buy a boat and you find the one that best accommodates your family for $70,000. Let's assume taxes and fees are built into the final price. As of writing this section, a 7 year boat loan with excellent credit is 4.99%.

Boat Loan period:	7 years (84 months)
Monthly payment:	$989
Boat Loan amount paid:	-$70,000
Interest @ 4.99% paid:	-$13,079
Total Paid to Bank:	**-$83,079**
Boat value after 7 years:	+$20,000
Total Loss(interest & Depreciation):	**-$63,079**

Again, I'm not trying to discourage anyone from buying a boat. I know that most people buy luxuries based on if they can afford the monthly payment. Rarely do they run the real numbers and a dealer certainly doesn't want you to see the total damage. Now take these numbers and imagine running this boat purchase through your specialized plan. You would have possession of the $83,079 back in your account and a $20,000 boat to sell for a total of $103,079 for the next purchase or if you are not wanting another boat, money to add towards your retirement.

Now imagine buying a rental property or family cabin or any asset that goes up in value. The numbers only get better plus you continue to earn interest internally as if the money were never gone. Any money you generate from the sale of a car or boat or RV or investment property is yours to keep!

The smart way to save for college

A common reason for purchasing these policies over the last 20 years has been for a smarter way of saving and paying for college. According to Limra, an insurance research firm, of all of the millions and millions of cash value policies in force in America today, 20% of them were purchased just for sending children to college.

These plans are an excellent way to save up money for a child's education. The most obvious, as you can guess, is while the funds are paying for college, they are still earning internally as if they had not been handed over to the university. However, this is also an excellent way to help children understand money and save for their own education.

A policy that could be used for college could be purchased on the child and gifted to him or her at a later date. It could also be purchased on the parent where both parent and child can fund the policy together. Who values their education more, the child that worked to pay for all or some of it or the one that it's just handed to?

What a great way to financially educate your child as a part of their total education.

As I share this strategy with parents who already own 529 college saving plans, their first question is can I transfer the money from the 529 and instead use an insurance contract? The answer is, not without cancelling the 529 plan which may or may not have fees to do so. With a 529 plan you are limited in where you can invest the money. You are limited by the fact that the money in the plan can ONLY be used for schooling. If you have a child that does not end up going to college, then you have to take a penalty and fee or sign up for night classes yourself. That money is only available for schooling costs.

However, people can and have stopped contributing to a 529 plan if their child still has time before starting college to start funding an insurance contract. The money in your insurance contract is protected against market loss, premature death, if the child decides not to attend college and it continues to earn interest until you or the child pays back the funds. This is the smarter way to fund a college education.

Being smart and strategic with your money does not give you license to be reckless. The money is yours to use and you will come out ahead by financing your own purchases, but only if you pay yourself back like you would the bank. Once you start retirement you can change the way you pay or not pay at all, but during the accumulation phase of your life, stay true to the concept and pay yourself back. This is a strategy to amplify your wealth by making each dollar do more than it could being used in the traditional ways we have been taught.

5. Real life examples

Almost a year ago I received a phone call from an insurance client from many years back. He is a successful eye doctor on the East Coast. After working in someone else's clinic for the first 10 years of his career, he was ready to move on and open his own practice. He and his wife were electric with excitement, but they couldn't get the financing from the bank. After reviewing his policy, how it worked and the cash value he had accumulated, it became obvious that he could finance some of his new practice with his insurance money and the rest from the bank. The bank loved the idea and because he needed less of a loan from them, the numbers made sense on their end. I'm happy to say this doctor is now his own boss, running his own eye care practice. I was thrilled to be a part of the solution but he is the reason for his own success.

Last year I had one of my favorite clients come to me with questions about how to use her cash value for flipping a piece of real estate. She had been looking at a hard money loan that carried loan terms of 12% APR plus 1% on the front and 2% on the back end. It was very expensive money! Meanwhile she had close to $130,000 liquid in her insurance account that could be borrowed at 5%. If this hadn't been a phone conversation, I'm almost certain she would have kissed me. She was ecstatic when she heard the news.

The loan was requested after filling out a 2 page form and the money was moved to her bank account 7 days later. I didn't hear from her for many months. Then one day I got a call that she had completed the project and turned a profit. Her policy continued to earn 5% interest while she used the money, but better than that, she made a 20% profit on the piece of real estate. With all of her money back in her insurance contract, she then had to figure out what to do with her 20% gain. Not a bad problem to have!

When I learned about the tax advantages, safety, growth potential and loan arrangements of these contracts, the first people I sat down with to share the concept with were my parents. I knew at some point they would want to retire comfortably and I would play a part in taking care of them. To my great surprise, my parents had each owned one of these insurance contracts for over 20 years.

They had been safely growing their money tax-free without a single year of losses for two decades. I was so happy to learn this and see the amount of money they had accumulated. Those plans have continued to earn every single year since I learned of their existence. My parents were prepared for retirement and to leave their children and grandchildren a legacy of smart money planning and tax-free inheritance.

Tow Truck Case Study

After working with many tow truck drivers and business owners, I've come to realize just how hard the towing business is. Long days, hot days, cold days, people up in your face days. One client's wife recently told me about the day her husband had someone pull a gun on him to try to get his car back.

Well I want to get up in your face, but in a good way. A way that will protect you from losing money. A way that will allow you to legally avoid taxes. A way that will turn your tow truck into a retirement money making machine. A way to recover the money you spend on truck purchases and have that money end up back in your personal possession.

Most business owners eventually get good at making money. Most even get better at finding ways to lower their taxes. Most however, don't figure out how to build solid retirement plans or learn how to make their money work for them in two places. With a properly built insurance contract, you can do everything I just mentioned above.

What I want you to walk away with today is that you already need life insurance to cover your family, lost income if you died, the business expenses and debt you might carry. But what if you could use this tool and some strategy to build a large tax-free nest egg that gave you access to capital when you need it and you could avoid the major expenses of working with a bank? What I am about to share with you will never be taught by banks or Wall Street yet they employ this strategy in their own businesses.

I want to show you an example of a tow truck owner in his early 40's that puts $15,000 away for JUST 5 years. We call this capitalizing or building up your business. Just like you didn't walk into instant success with your towing business, this plan needs some time to get up and running. As you can see based on the contribution and a 6.5% average growth rate, this owner could place money for 5 years and then never contribute another dime to his account.

This should give him around $287,785 at age 70. This money is tax-free and will continue to grow in value. The death benefit has also grown in value over the years. At age 70 he has nearly 5 times more money than the average baby boomer retiring today.

Age	End of policy year	Premium outlay	Accumulation value	Cash value	Death benefit	Accumulation value	Cash value	Death benefit
42	1	$15,000.00	$13,055	$3,665	$376,451	$13,355	$3,964	$376,751
43	2	$15,000.00	$26,731	$17,454	$390,127	$27,653	$18,375	$391,049
44	3	$15,000.00	$41,052	$31,894	$404,448	$42,955	$33,797	$406,351
45	4	$15,000.00	$56,042	$47,005	$419,438	$59,330	$50,292	$422,726
46	5	$15,000.00	$71,731	$62,821	$435,127	$76,850	$67,939	$440,246
47	6	$0.00	$73,640	$64,857	$437,036	$80,769	$71,986	$444,165
48	7	$0.00	$75,584	$66,931	$438,980	$84,917	$76,264	$448,313
49	8	$0.00	$77,578	$70,368	$440,974	$89,324	$82,114	$452,720
50	9	$0.00	$79,611	$73,843	$443,007	$93,995	$88,228	$457,391
51	10	$0.00	$81,664	$77,340	$445,060	$98,930	$94,605	$462,326
52	11	$0.00	$83,716	$80,834	$447,112	$104,124	$101,242	$467,520
53	12	$0.00	$85,743	$84,304	$449,139	$109,574	$108,135	$472,970
54	13	$0.00	$88,534	$88,534	$451,930	$116,098	$116,098	$479,494
55	14	$0.00	$91,276	$91,276	$454,672	$122,915	$122,915	$486,311
56	15	$0.00	$93,945	$93,945	$457,341	$130,023	$130,023	$493,419
57	16	$0.00	$96,528	$96,528	$459,924	$137,436	$137,436	$500,832
58	17	$0.00	$99,028	$99,028	$462,424	$145,184	$145,184	$508,580
59	18	$0.00	$101,440	$101,440	$464,836	$153,291	$153,291	$516,687
60	19	$0.00	$103,723	$103,723	$467,119	$161,747	$161,747	$525,143
61	20	$0.00	$106,124	$106,124	$469,520	$170,835	$170,835	$534,231
62	21	$0.00	$108,649	$108,649	$472,045	$180,602	$180,602	$543,998
63	22	$0.00	$111,305	$111,305	$474,701	$191,100	$191,100	$554,496
64	23	$0.00	$114,098	$114,098	$477,494	$202,382	$202,382	$565,778
65	24	$0.00	$117,036	$117,036	$480,432	$214,507	$214,507	$577,903
66	25	$0.00	$120,126	$120,126	$483,522	$227,539	$227,539	$590,935
67	26	$0.00	$123,298	$123,298	$486,694	$241,467	$241,467	$604,863
68	27	$0.00	$126,337	$126,337	$489,733	$256,134	$256,134	$619,530
69	28	$0.00	$129,201	$129,201	$492,597	$271,562	$271,562	$634,958
70	29	$0.00	$131,860	$131,860	$495,256	$287,785	$287,785	$651,181

However, it gets better and here's how. Once you have capitalized your plan or built up cash value, you can borrow against the plan and use that money to buy equipment, expand or buy a new truck. For this example, let's say you buy a new truck every 4 years. While you are borrowing against your plan, the money in your plan continues to grow as if it were never gone. It's the only financial vehicle that allows this.

As you pay yourself back, you will ultimately end up placing more money back in your account, but the real genius I show people is when you sell your truck, drop that money into your plan. Here's why, that lump sum of money enters the policy and increases the accumulation value inside your plan. You can then borrow it right back out to purchase the next truck. Loans take 5 minutes and 1 piece of paper. Nothing is simpler! Can you say that about getting a loan from a bank?

Age	End of policy year	Premium outlay	Interest/ Loan credits	Interest Bonus credit	Policy charges	Loan charges	Accumulation value	Cash value	Death benefit
42	1	$15,000.00	$847	$127	$2,620	$0	$13,355	$3,964	$376,751
43	2	$15,000.00	$1,713	$257	$2,672	$0	$27,653	$18,375	$391,049
44	3	$15,000.00	$2,640	$396	$2,734	$0	$42,955	$33,797	$406,351
45	4	$15,000.00	$3,633	$545	$2,803	$0	$59,330	$50,292	$422,726
46	5	$15,000.00	$4,694	$704	$2,878	$0	$76,850	$67,939	$440,246
47	6	$0.00	$4,933	$740	$1,754	$0	$80,769	$71,986	$444,165
48	7	$0.00	$5,186	$778	$1,816	$0	$84,917	$76,264	$448,313
49	8	$0.00	$5,454	$818	$1,865	$0	$89,324	$82,114	$452,720
50	9	$30,000.00	$6,985	$863	$4,328	$0	$122,844	$117,077	$486,240
51	10	$0.00	$7,914	$1,187	$2,010	$0	$129,936	$125,611	$493,332
		$105,000.00							
52	11	$0.00	$8,371	$1,256	$2,115	$0	$137,448	$134,566	$500,844
53	12	$0.00	$8,855	$1,328	$2,243	$0	$145,388	$143,949	$508,784
54	13	$30,000.00	$10,693	$1,410	$2,801	$0	$184,690	$184,690	$548,086
55	14	$0.00	$11,942	$1,791	$1,789	$0	$196,635	$196,635	$560,031
56	15	$0.00	$12,711	$1,907	$1,999	$0	$209,253	$209,253	$572,649
57	16	$0.00	$13,523	$2,029	$2,217	$0	$222,589	$222,589	$585,985
58	17	$30,000.00	$15,682	$2,159	$3,627	$0	$266,802	$266,802	$630,198
59	18	$0.00	$17,249	$2,587	$2,638	$0	$284,000	$284,000	$647,396
60	19	$0.00	$18,358	$2,754	$2,886	$0	$302,227	$302,227	$665,623
61	20	$0.00	$19,543	$2,931	$2,886	$0	$321,816	$321,816	$685,212
		$165,000.00							
62	21	$30,000.00	$22,115	$3,124	$4,086	$0	$372,969	$372,969	$736,365
63	22	$0.00	$24,141	$3,621	$2,886	$0	$397,846	$397,846	$761,242
64	23	$0.00	$25,758	$3,864	$2,886	$0	$424,582	$424,582	$787,978
65	24	$0.00	$27,496	$4,124	$2,886	$0	$453,318	$453,318	$816,714
66	25	$35,000.00	$30,878	$4,406	$4,286	$0	$519,316	$519,316	$882,712
67	26	$0.00	$33,651	$5,048	$2,961	$0	$555,054	$555,054	$918,450
68	27	$0.00	$35,964	$5,395	$3,250	$0	$593,162	$593,162	$956,558
69	28	$0.00	$38,430	$5,764	$3,573	$0	$633,783	$633,783	$997,179
70	29	$35,000.00	$42,572	$6,160	$5,317	$0	$712,199	$712,199	$1,075,595

Every 4 years this business owner drops the extra money from his or her sold truck in to their plan. They then borrow against that for the next truck. As you do this it bumps your value up and will ultimately result in more money in your tax-free bucket.

9 years into the plan, I show this owner drop $30,000 into their plan. Four years goes by and he or she needs a new truck so they sell the current truck and dump the $30,000 in before purchasing the next truck. They do this a few more times. By 25 years from now, trucks will probably be more expensive so you will pay more but when you sell in 4 years so will the person that buys it from you so I show $35,000 going into the plan. Finally, at age 70, you sell off the final truck and dump one last amount of money into your plan before retiring, selling the business or handing it off to your children. The plan should have around $712,199 of tax-free money for your retirement years. That's a pretty significant increase in your nest egg just by buying the trucks you would have bought any way from your plan and then dumping the money back in when it sells. In this case study, the difference was **$424,414** more. This increase is worth taking the time to understand these plans.

Plus you still get to write off the interest and depreciation. I'll share how when we speak. This examples should serve as an example to all business owners of the equipment they could buy and finance through their contract. This client just happens to use his plan for tow truck. Don't get hung up if you aren't a tow truck driver.

Now I'd like to ask a few simple questions that have very revealing answers:

Do you plan to save money and retire one day?

Would you like to legally avoid paying taxes in the future?

During your business career, are you going to purchase several trucks or cars to run your business or get to work?

Has anyone ever shown you a smarter way to buy trucks and cars or equipment from an insurance contract?

Regardless of owning one of my plans or not, are you going to buy trucks or cars or other major purchases?

At age 70 would you rather have $287,785 or $712,199?

No bank is going to show you how to buy your tow trucks or cars this smarter way. No bank is going to encourage you to save in an insurance contract instead of with them. No bank is going to show you how to legally avoid taxes. And no bank is going to show you how to recover the money you lose to interest and depreciation and then how to properly dump the money you got from selling your truck or car into a plan that will grow your retirement.

Well, I am not a bank! I will show you how to do all this just like I have shown all my clients. Just like I have personally done for a decade. There is a smarter way to behave with money that helps you keep more and have more. Time passes the same for all of us, but we all end up with different results. Let's get you the best results with the money you were already going to save for yourself and the money you were going to spend on your business.

Now, imagine running multiple trucks or cars through this plan. I'll let you in on a secret, the result is more money and freedom during retirement. This can be on any type of company equipment, cars, trucks or major purchases.

Airplane Business - Case Study

This strategy will leave you flying high and in first class. I'm fortunate to know many of the brightest people in the insurance world. I was blessed to learn about the Become Your Own Banker strategy right from best-selling Author, Nelson Nash.

Last week I was able to interview someone that has been involved with cash value life insurance for a long time. He shared a story with me and gave me permission to share it with my readers. I've changed a few details to keep things anonymous but I heard it from his own lips.

This friend is obsessed with planes and flying. He's also a big fan of being his own source of financing to recover the money he spends on major purchases. His major purchase has been an airplane. Yes, he has used this strategy for other, smaller purchases but this one was pretty unique.

This friend is partners in a flight school where they teach students how to fly and collect the hours of practice required to become a private or commercial airline pilot. He loves his job. Not long ago these two partners had the opportunity to buy several airplanes but couldn't secure the financing from the bank. On a new plane you can usually get a 20 year loan at 6%. On a used plane, you had better have cash or be willing to pay 15% interest on top of collateral equal to the plane purchase price.

The used planes he and his partner were looking at easily generate over $100,000 in revenue even though they are older. So instead of passing on these planes, he was able to dip into the insurance contract he owns as a source of capital. He had set up a plan for himself 16 years earlier that had grown quite well.

Year	Age	Total Premium	Dividend	Premium Outlay	Cum. Premium Outlay	Total Cash Value	Change in Total Cash Value	Change in CV Less Prem. Outlay	Total Death Benefit w/out Div	Total Death Benefit
1	31	18,000	184	18,000	18,000	6,948	6,948	-11,052	1,780,207	1,780,391
2	32	18,000	391	18,000	36,000	14,876	7,927	-10,073	1,780,207	1,780,598
3	33	18,000	608	18,000	54,000	31,233	16,357	-1,643	1,780,207	1,780,815
4	34	18,000	1,036	18,000	72,000	50,066	18,833	833	1,780,207	1,781,243
5	35	18,000	1,541	18,000	90,000	70,131	20,065	2,065	1,780,207	1,781,748
6	36	18,000	2,023	18,000	108,000	91,448	21,317	3,317	1,780,207	1,782,230
7	37	18,000	3,251	18,000	126,000	114,769	23,321	5,321	1,780,207	1,783,458
8	38	18,000	3,804	18,000	144,000	139,515	24,746	6,746	1,780,207	1,784,011
9	39	18,000	4,412	18,000	162,000	165,748	26,233	8,233	1,780,207	1,784,619
10	40	18,000	5,068	18,000	180,000	193,586	27,838	9,838	1,780,207	1,785,275
11	41	18,000	5,750	18,000	198,000	221,691	28,105	10,105	1,780,207	1,785,957
12	42	18,000	6,488	18,000	216,000	251,514	29,824	11,824	1,780,207	1,786,695
13	43	18,000	7,281	18,000	234,000	283,140	31,626	13,626	1,780,207	1,787,488
14	44	18,000	8,124	18,000	252,000	316,655	33,515	15,515	1,780,207	1,788,331
15	45	18,000	9,018	18,000	270,000	352,156	35,501	17,501	1,780,207	1,789,225
16	46	18,000	9,985	18,000	288,000	389,781	37,625	19,625	1,780,207	1,790,192
17	47	18,000	11,021	18,000	306,000	429,699	39,918	21,918	1,780,207	1,791,228
18 [1]	48	18,000	12,086	18,000	324,000	472,022	42,324	24,324	1,780,207	1,792,293
19	49	18,000	13,060	18,000	342,000	516,809	44,786	26,786	1,824,678	1,837,738
20	50	18,000	14,114	18,000	360,000	564,160	47,351	29,351	1,887,499	1,901,613
21	51	18,000	15,252	18,000	378,000	614,178	50,018	32,018	1,951,359	1,966,611
22	52	18,000	16,501	18,000	396,000	667,012	52,835	34,835	2,016,373	2,032,874
23	53	18,000	17,881	18,000	414,000	722,773	55,761	37,761	2,082,714	2,100,595
24	54	18,000	19,317	18,000	432,000	781,574	58,801	40,801	2,150,596	2,169,913
25	55	18,000	20,851	18,000	450,000	843,475	61,900	43,900	2,220,019	2,240,870

At age 46 he has nearly $390,000 in cash he can borrow at 5% interest and set up his own pay back schedule. So this is what he has done! The plane cost him $80,000 and he plans to pay it back and depreciate it over a 20 year time frame.

If he had been able to get a bank loan he would have had a 240 month repayment plan with a $573 a month payment. Over that time period he would have lost $57,555 to interest. I typically like to show what would have been lost to depreciation but that is hard to do on an airplane and 20 years. Planes tend to hold value better than cars because they aren't made in great numbers like cars are so we'll leave it at $57,555 lost to interest.

$573 paid for 240 months is $137,520 for an $80,000 plane. So, instead of paying that money away from himself, he will have that amount back in his possession by paying himself instead of a bank. Plus, the money he borrowed against from his insurance contract will continue to grow and compound uninterrupted.

Had this friend deprived his $80,000 from earning interest to pay cash for the plane, he would have missed out on this money growing to $212,263. I got this by having $80,000 compound annually at 5% interest for 20 years. Paying cash is typically worse than financing a loan. Uninterrupted compounding interest coupled with not losing interest and depreciation on major purchases is a lethal combination. So use it to your advantage!

Your estimated monthly payments are $573 and you will pay $57,555 in interest over the life of the loan.

Apply for Loan

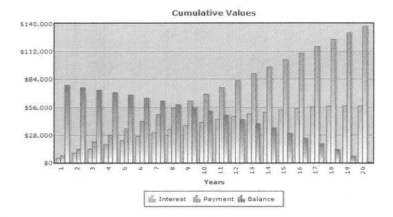

$80,000 loan at 5% for 20 yrs

However, understanding the tax code and wanting to be smart with his money, the friend plans to buy the plane himself and then lease it to his LLC at 15% interest. The business gets to write off the interest and the depreciation and the friend gets to put the additional money back into his account. This is all legal and it's the same rate he would have paid a bank to secure financing on a used plane. This payment will be higher but the business makes enough to cover the lease and be profitable. This pays off his $80,000 loan at nearly double the rate and puts all that extra money back in his pocket. He will max out this policy eventually and have to buy another plan. What a great problem to have.

Your estimated monthly payments are $1,053 and you will pay $172,824 in interest over the life of the loan.

Apply for Loan

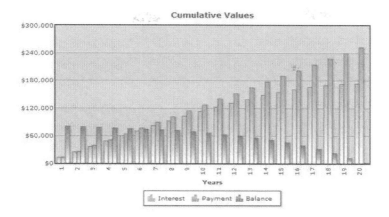

$80,000 lease loan at 15% for 20 years

This friend stands to come out far ahead financially by purchasing his airplane for his business through his insurance contract. Because of his diligent savings, he will be able to take advantage of an opportunity he couldn't have imagined 16 years earlier. He also has enough money to purchase 3 planes and leave himself a cushion of emergency money. Now multiply these numbers by 3 planes and you can see why this friend was excited to share his idea with me. I was excited for him.

Most people will have a greater need for financing in their life time then they will be able to save. So why not save and be your own best customer on good loans instead of giving away all your money to the bank or risking it on Wall Street? If you are a business owner, you know you hate handing all this money off to the bank. Not only can you be smarter for your business, but you can stuff more money into your pocket.

Let me show you how a properly built plan can be an incredible money maker for you down the road. I don't know what opportunities or emergencies will come your way during your life, but they come and things turn out best for those that are prepared.

Don't get hung up in you don't own an airplane. This is an example to show the creativity of these plans and how they can put a ton of money in your pocket along the way. 16 years ago this friend wasn't a pilot and had no dream of owning multiple planes, but he did want to retire so he started a plan.

It was his preparation and access to money and affordable lending that made this possible. So get started and let the future come to you as a prepared person. Opportunity always comes knocking and works out best for those ready and able to answer the call.

For over a dozen more case studies and real life client examples, check out my blog by visiting www.YourBridgePlan.com.

6. 10 reasons to be your own source of financing through specially built insurance plan:

1. You can borrow money from your contract as soon as you have adequate cash value built up.
2. The government, your employer, or anyone else can no longer tell you how to use your money.
3. Your contract is protected against market loss.
4. You can borrow your money for any reason. No qualifying. No credit checks.
5. When you borrow money from your contract it continues to earn as if you hadn't taken the money out. It allows you to earn interest in two places. No other financial vehicle allows this.
6. Recover money you would have lost to interest, depreciation, business start-up and education.
7. Your contract can earn decent interest to keep up with inflation and the rising cost of living.
8. You can use your money for unforeseen life events like a new baby, medical bills, etc.
9. You contract values will never slide backwards because of the economy.
10. Your contract earnings grow tax-free. You can access your money tax-free and your beneficiary receives the death benefit income tax-free.

Plans MUST be built correctly

The benefits of these plans come from the way the insurance companies have structured the contracts to allow you to build cash, legally avoid taxes and borrow against the policy for purchases or retirement. However, the **POWER** of these contracts comes from how they are designed by the agent. Done correctly and for the benefit of the client, they are incredible. Done incorrectly or for the benefit of the agent and they become disastrous. Who you use and how it is built is critical!

For many years I have been training insurance agents on how to design and use these private contracts for their clients. I'm continually shocked to learn how few agents know about these plans let alone understand how to properly design them to a client's advantage. Most know nothing! Some know just enough to be dangerous and only a select few really, really get it.

Even scarier is that I have never had an insurance company educate me on how to use these plans the way I design them. I had to learn these strategies from mentors, playing with the software for hours and owning these contracts myself. In fact, when I design a contract for a client, the insurance company's first response to me upon submitting the client's paperwork is that if I built it a more traditional way it would pay me more money. I simply ask if the way I built the contract is legal and within the guidelines of the IRS rules. They of course tell me yes. So I build it my way to maximize growth and liquidity for the client. Having an agent that owns these plans themselves is a must. You don't want the blind leading the blind.

There is an approach to designing these plans that truly benefits the client. I'll discuss in greater detail soon. What I want to show you is how to create a savings plan that behaves like an investment plan and does it without compounding your future tax burden because your money grows tax-free.

As I mentioned earlier in the chapter there are two main products for building these programs to work the way I have been describing. The first is a properly built dividend paying insurance contract. These grow like clockwork each and every year like they have for over 100 years. The dividend is not guaranteed like the interest rate but the groups I use have never missed a dividend payment. The example will be on a 40 year old male in standard health contributing $600 a month until age 65.

The second type uses the indexing strategy. Like the former, your funds are protected against market loss. Your interest rate is calculated and credited based upon the performance of the stock market index you linked to for the year. You can change your index allocation strategy each year if you feel one index may outperform another. This strategy has potential to earn higher returns so there is some speculation to what return you might get. Most groups have averaged over 8% for the past 25 years but for the example illustration I will be using a 6.5% average growth rate to be conservative. The index strategy example will be on a 40 year old male in standard health contributing $700 a month until age 65. I purposely used different dollar amounts because I want you to see this as a concept. That said, the numbers in both examples are real numbers.

With both strategies, I will be showing you a side by side comparison of a traditional plan compared to the way I build contracts. The outcome becomes fairly obvious very quickly. Math doesn't lie. I build contracts this way because it maximizes growth for the client and it's the right thing to do.

Choose your mentor wisely

Have you ever been at an industry conference or in a room with people that do the same things as you, only to realize some of these people don't know what you know?

Recently I volunteered to help my son's school with an outside activity. Towards the end of the day I was speaking with another student's mother that I have known for 3 years. She was asking me a few money questions and I was answering them. We got on the topic of taxes, safety and loans.

I was sharing with her about these incredible insurance contracts that can be used to build a tax-free retirement, how they are protected against market loss, grow every year and how she could use the money to be her own source of financing for real estate and cars. If you've read my books and the other articles on my blog, you know I am talking about a properly designed cash value insurance contract.

I started sharing how the loans works and how my wife and I have used them for real estate and for our cars. She was fascinated by the whole thing and had several really great questions. She asked me to drop off a copy of my best-selling book so she and her husband could read it over.

About this time, another dad we had been volunteering with interrupted to ask me a question about being his own source of financing on cars. As we talked and I shared more information, I could see how interested and curious he was becoming. He had some great questions, too.

Then the big shocker happened. I told him this was a specially designed permanent insurance contract. He looked at my like a deer in head lights. He said he had never heard of this before and had no idea these types of plans could work this way. He even confessed to owning one but wondered if it had been structured correctly when it was set up.

I then asked him what he did for work. He told me he sells life insurance. I could feel my eyes get wide as I processed the information but also tried not to look at this gentleman like he was a total idiot. I asked him how long he had been in the industry. He told me for almost a decade.

I dug a little deeper on the groups he was working with. Yep, they have this type of plan. I asked him about training, books he had read and how he built plans. He had read no books and had no training.

Here I was standing face to face with the very type of agent I try to educate people to avoid. Here was the agent that made other agents look bad because he knew only enough to be dangerous but look helpful. Here I was shocked that he was doing as well as he was while unknowingly leading his clients down the wrong path or at least the longer path.

Who you work with matters. Who you choose as a mentor matters. How a plan is built matters. The company that honors the contract and will be your lifelong partner matters. Most people don't know what they don't know so they either sign up with this guy and find out later they have an inferior plan. Or they never find out and don't know the difference. Worse is that this guy presents plans that look bad and perform worse and make those of us that have worked hard to build great plans look bad by association.

If the agent you are working with doesn't own these type of contracts or understand them inside and out, please walk away. You are being blindly lead by the blind. Let me show you how I build a superior contract and how to use your contract to your advantage.

Don't get caught with the deer in head lights look when you find out the mentor you chose doesn't understand how to use these contracts, doesn't personally own these contracts and has no real world experience with the lending power of these contracts.

Keys points of the dividend paying illustration (see table below)

I've added circles around key points I want to point out. We will discuss from top to bottom and I will address the column by name to avoid confusion. The first numbers I want to bring to your attention are found in the dividend column for the traditional plan. You can see there are no dividends in the first few years of the plan compared with my plan which starts paying dividends from year one. You will also notice that the traditional plan has little or no cash value in the first two years compared to immediate cash value in my plan. This early cash value can be borrowed against as soon as it is in your plan.

Now turn your attention to year 10. At this point you have contributed $72,000 towards the insurance contracts death benefit and cash account. In the traditional plan I've pointed out that your money has only grown to $65,186. While my plan has $81,183 which means it is well past breakeven and is now starting to pick up growth. Some look at this as having the death benefit paid for and the plan starts to accelerate as a cash accumulation vehicle.

25 years into the contract or age 65 of this man, he has contributed $180,000 to his contract. At this point you can see that he no longer makes additional contributions. He can if he likes, but it isn't required of him. The traditional contract has $286,462 in cash value whereas my plan has $313,352. That's $26,890 more. Remember we placed the same amount of money for the same amount of time in both contracts but one has cash value faster, dividends earlier and a larger amount of money for retirement.

40 yr old male	Dividend Paying Whole Life	$600 / month contribution		Traditional Plan Cash Value			My Plan Cash Value
Age	Policy year	Total Premium Contribution	Dividend On Top of Interest	Cash Value	Dividend On Top of Interest		Cash Value
41	1	$7200	$0	$0	$129		$4,748
42	2	$14,400	$0	$308	$275		$10,245
45	5	$36000	$709	$20,651	$926		$32,904
50	10	$72,000	$2,167	$65,186	$2,295		$81,183
55	15	$108,000	$3,781	$120,308	$4,080		$144,966
60	20	$144,000	$6,086	$192,699	$6,582		$229,228
65	25	$180,000	$9,080	$286,462	$9,187		$313,352
75	35	$180,000	$14,363	$489,280	$15,710		$535,171
85	45	$180,000	$24,710	$793,194	$27,028		$867,591
95	55	$180,000	$35,437	$1,191,292	$38,761		$1,303,028

Key points of the indexing plan (see table below)

The first numbers I want to bring to your attention are found in the cash value column for the traditional plan. You can see there is no cash value in the first few years of the plan compared to my plan which has cash value from year one. This early cash value can be borrowed against as soon as it is in your plan. The main discrepancy between the two is the traditional plan is built as an insurance plan whereas mine is built to be a cash building, tax-free machine for retirement and financing purchases faster.

There is a way to build these contracts that most agents are unwilling to do because it drops their commission significantly. Some will even walk away from a client before making these changes. I prefer to give the very best plan to the client and to their referrals. Plus I sleep well at night knowing I put forth my very best plan.

Now turn your attention to year 10. At this point he has contributed $84,000 towards the insurance contracts death benefit and cash account. In a traditional plan I've pointed out that he only has $72,879. While my plan shows $92,579 which means it is well past breakeven and is now starting to pick up growth. Some look at this as having the death benefit paid for and the plan starts to accelerate as a cash accumulation vehicle.

25 years into the contract or age 65 of this man, he has contributed $210,000 to the contract. At this point you can see that he no longer makes additional contributions. He can if he likes but it isn't required of him. The traditional contract has $360,040 in cash value whereas my plan has $453,066. That's $93,026 more. Remember, we placed the same amount of money for the same amount of time in both contracts assuming the same 6.5% potential growth average, but mine has cash value faster and more money.

If the client didn't need to access the money or chose to live off his 401k money for the first 10 years of retirement by age 75 he could have $916,565 compared to $638,091. That's a $278,474 difference between the traditional plan and my plan. The difference between a traditional policy and the contracts I build is incredible; faster access to money and a lot more money. Creating a plan that gives a client hundreds of thousands of tax-free dollars more is the way these contracts should be built.

40 yr old male	Indexing Plan	$700 / month contribution	Traditional Plan Cash Value	My Plan Cash Value
Age	Policy year	Total Premium Contribution	Cash Value	Cash Value
41	1	$8,400	0	$6,666
42	2	$16,800	0	$13,805
45	5	$42,000	$19,977	$38,363
50	10	$84,000	$72,879	$92,579
55	15	$126,000	$146,236	$173,603
60	20	$168,000	$235,688	$289,044
65	25	$210,000	$360,040	$453,066
75	35	$210,000	$638,091	$916,565
85	45	$210,000	$1,035,333	$1,855,015
95	55	$210,000	$1,098,375	$3,655,099

Income example (see table below)

I'm only going to show an example of taking income in retirement using the indexing strategy. They are so similar that I trust you will see the concept and understand the math. In this example I'm going to assume the person retires at age 65 and stops contributing to their plan. Now they are ready to use the plan to supplement their pension, Social Security or other investment income streams. There are a few ways to take money from a plan – by withdrawal or through policy loans. Some people like to draw money down as a withdrawal until it equals the amount of premium they contributed and then switch to loans.

This is because you can draw down to your base amount of contribution without paying tax since the premiums were originally paid with after tax dollars you contributed. Every dollar after that still needs to be taxed so clients switch over to loans since loans can't be taxed and loans are paid off at death by the death benefit.

For this example, we are just going to demonstrate loans. As you can see in the 66th year this plan is predicted to pay $43,414 until age 120. Although most people pass away in their early 80s, I prefer to show examples of not running out of money. You will notice in the cash value column, the cash value is starting to lower in value. This is because as you take a loan, you no longer have that amount of collateral to loan against. Your death benefit will also lower each year in anticipation of these loans being paid off upon your death. That way your family isn't saddled with a huge unpaid loan.

Let's assume you live to the age of 85 and drew money off your plan for 20 years. That means you lived off $868,280 of tax-free money from your plan. Remember, you only contributed $210,000. That means you took more than four times the amount of money out of the plan as you contributed and didn't have to pay a dime of taxes. Plus, this plan still has $311,986 in death benefit to pass on income tax-free to your family. That's $868,280 during your lifetime plus $311,986 in death benefit. You derived $1,180,266 from a program to which you only contributed $210,000. There is nothing like these plans on the market. BRILLIANT!

40 yr old male	Indexing Plan	$700 / month contribution		My Plan Cash Value
Age	Policy year	Total Premium Contribution	Income Stream	Cash Value
60	20	$168,000	$0	$289,044
65	25	$210,000	$0	$453,066
66	26	$210,000	$43,414	$440,284
67	27	$210,000	$43,414	$427,350
68	28	$210,000	$43,414	$414,254
69	29	$210,000	$43,414	$401,023
70	30	$210,000	$43,414	$387,692
75	35	$210,000	$43,414	$322,335
85	45	$210,000	$43,414	$225,353

Compare this to whatever you have in your 401k, upon death, it is taxed and the leftovers are passed on. The same goes for your IRA. It too is taxed and the leftovers are passed on. Depleting your 401k, IRA, savings or CDs means you have less money each year for yourself and your heirs. Plus those accounts still have to pass through Uncle Sam's greedy hands.

This may be fairly obvious but to get the equivalent of $43,414 out of a 401k or IRA you must pull nearly $53,000 out per year, assuming a 28% tax bracket. This means you must have significantly more in a 401k or IRA than an insurance contract because you still have to pay Uncle Sam his share first before you receive your share. This also means you are depleting your 401k or IRA at a faster rate because of the larger amount.

One overlooked strategy for those that own an insurance contract and a retirement account like a 401k or IRA is using the two together to make sure you don't outlive your money. To do this most people can provide their insurance contract an additional 10 years of compound growth by living off their taxable accounts first. There are no required minimum distributions with an insurance contract. This buys your insurance contract more time while your taxable accounts provide you income. The result from delaying payments for 10 years is usually about twice as much annual income from your insurance contract.

I once heard that we are only as tall as the shoulders we stand upon. This is referencing the quality of our lives and the opportunities we have access to, based on how well our parents or grandparents did. The hope as a parent is that the next generation is smarter, richer and better than us. Having a system you can confidently save in, earn a good return on your money with, legally avoid taxes, have access to your funds at any age and earn interest on used funds as if they were never gone will ultimately allow you to have taller shoulders for the next generation to stand on. In the event that you die prematurely, that lump sum of tax-free money is going to pass on to the next generation allowing them to stand on tall shoulders.

Most people purchase a policy on themselves. However, you can own a policy on anyone you have insurable interest in. I've had clients buy a policy on their children for college planning. I've had clients in bad health buy on a spouse or child. I've seen grandparent co-own a contract on a grandchild.

Being tall for yourself allows you to see ahead on the maze of life. It allows you to see the end from the beginning, move forward with confidence, avoid dead ends and back tracking. It also allows you to model an incredible way of building wealth strategically for your children and grandchildren while providing for them financially in case you aren't here to help. This strategy is worthy of your time and attention. It has certainly blessed my life as a contract owner and many of my client's lives all across the country.

This chapter has attempted to articulate an incredible concept for growing money without the risk of losing, building truly tax-free wealth and how to make your dollar work in two place at once to provide you with more money down the road. However, the book alone should not be used to replace the knowledge of an experienced insurance agent. Agents connected to our office can walk you through your personal situation and show how this will lead to significantly more wealth in your future.

Make sure to check out www.yourbridgeplan.com for more examples, stories and videos.

7. LUMP SUM STRATEGY

I want to share one more idea with you that clients have loved. It's another way to grow your money without using life insurance. It also allows you to take advantage of the indexing strategy with a lump sum or one time placement of money. You can have the cake of Wall Street and eat it too without ever worrying about losing money.

I think the most remarkable part of the indexing strategy is the annual reset feature that locks in your gains. When I say lock in, I mean locked in. As in not going anywhere. The gains on your money are yours forever. They can't be taken away depending on how the market performs the following year. The worst that can happen is a zero. In this case zero is your hero and you'll see later in this chapter why I say this.

This strategy is not built for income, although you could take income down the road. It's not built for moving money around and rebalancing every quarter, although the company does that for you. This strategy is purely built for growth on your money.

The groups we use have access to some of the best talent in the investment world because they can afford these money managers. These money managers aren't driven by commissions or paid a percentage for how many assets they have under management. This isn't about skimming fees off a client's portfolio. They are salaried and bonused based on one goal – increasing the customer's bottom line. Wouldn't it be nice to be the central focus of an <u>investment strategy</u> and not the central focus of a <u>marketing campaign</u>?

The company is only paid when the manager increases your portfolio. So if these managers grow your money, they get paid. If they don't grow your money, the company will guarantee that you as the customer don't lose, but the company makes nothing for the year. This puts the incentive on growth and not just on holding client's money.

In my other books I have an entire chapter dedicated to how Wall Street makes their money on fees. Whether your money increases or decreases, they get paid. I don't mind people earning when they've done something good for me, but it I have a loss or a break even, it bothers me to see someone get paid. The incentive should be on growth and with this strategy the incentive is in the right place.

This strategy grows when the market goes up with no cap or restriction on how much you can earn. I've seen zeros; I've seen double digits and everything in between. You can use cash, family trust money, old 401Ks, IRAs or Roth IRAs.

If you could earn market returns, but have losses eliminated, wouldn't that simplify your understanding? We all want the highs of the market and to avoid the pain, lost sleep and stress of the years when the market drops. This strategy does it for you.

If you have a lump sum of money that isn't as protected as you'd like, isn't earning as much as you'd like or isn't as hands off as you'd like, then this strategy may be for you. As one of my favorite financial authors described this strategy, 'once you see how it can grow and protect your money, why would you grow your money any other way? It simply isn't worth the risk.'

So what is this mystery growth vehicle?

The program I am describing is a specialized type of growth focused annuity. There are several hundred types of annuities out there. Most I wouldn't touch with a 10 foot pole. I've been dealing with annuities since 2003 when I first learned about them. To be honest, I've hated them from the moment we met.

If you get the wrong annuity, you could very easily have just signed up for a decade's worth of headaches. There are annuities that pay you income until you die and then keep the difference. There are annuities that promise you a fixed rate of return until you start income and you're your account value never grows by another dollar. There are annuities that people bought because they promised returns higher than a CD and now a CD can out earn their contract.

I stayed away from annuities like these like they were a disease. That is until I was granted access to these specialized annuities that work on a spread and have uncapped earning potential. I had no idea they existed until a mega producer introduced me to the right person.

There are thousands of agents that will sell you a traditional annuity or a capped FIA (Fixed Indexed Annuity), but most of them don't have access to uncapped opportunities. Only the very best companies offer these programs and it is usually reserved for their top producers.

Protecting Against Losses

How would you like to never lose money again?

This question really hits home with people that lived through 2000-2002 when the market experienced 3 years of double digit losses back to back. Or the people that were in the stock market during the great recession when the stock market dropped by 52% and took five and a half years just to get back to break even. 2008 saw a 38% decrease on its own.

You only know how painful and damaging losses can be if you have experienced them.

There are many that started investing after 2009 and have ridden the longest bull market in history. They believe they are excellent investors, but they haven't been up against the kind of losses the majority of our country has lived through.

A rising tide lifts all ships and a sinking tide exposes who has been swimming naked. There is a way to rise with the tide and lock in your money before it all rush back out with a sinking market.

Having an annuity backed by a financially stable insurance company is like having a big fat insurance policy wrapped around your retirement account. Insurance companies are the most regulated financial institutions in the world. More than Wall Street and certainly more than banks. During the Great Depression the news reported that thousands of banks went under. During the Great Recession over 400 banks closed shop and most of Wall Street had to be bailed out by taxpayer money.

Because of reserves and conservative investments, insurance companies weathered these storms and continued to be a safe haven to the American people. They have maintained trust with clients during both World Wars and everything else thrown at them. They are a solid foundation you can trust to build on.

In 1933, Walt Disney's cartoon company put out a nine minute short film titled The 3 Little Pigs. Maybe you've seen it or know the story. In this short story, there is a big bad wolf with exceptionally powerful lungs, destroying the homes of those he comes in contact with. In the story he comes across three brother pigs that have all prepared homes of different strength.

The first brother builds his home out of straw. When life is good, he thinks and believes he has a strong house. When the wolf comes knocking, he soon finds out that his home is easily blown to the ground.

The second brother builds his home out of sticks. He feels he has built a strong home because wood is strong and reliable and everyone knows how reliable wood can be. However, this house made of sticks is no match for the lungs of the hungry wolf. With a few big blows, he is able to dismantle the stick home and send it crashing to the earth.

The two pigs run for their lives until they come to their brother's home. The final pig has built his home out of brick and mortar. The home has a firm foundation. As hard as the wolf tries, he can't blow the brick home down.

The truth is, we have many wolves that are after us and our money; market loss, management fees, low performance, fraud and scams and inflation to name just a few. If we aren't vigilant to the damage these wolves can do, we find our homes beaten up and wrecked. I believe the proper annuity is a solid foundation you can build on that won't be blown over now or in the future.

How strong is your financial plan now?

No one knows when the market will turn on you. It can't be predicted and the gurus on TV are paid because they are good entertainers and not because of their crystal ball reading abilities. Anyone that tells you they can predict the market is lying or wants your money.

Recently even Warren Buffet's group took a 28% loss on Kraft Stock. Facebook experienced an 18% stock drop in one day. I'm not saying the stock market is bad, because it can be very good. An annuity is simply an excellent way to tame Wall Street.

With the growth focused annuities, you get to participate in the upside of the stock market while eliminating the losses. I've seen double digit losses to the stock market result in a zero loss to annuity clients. I've seen a double digit increase be locked in, never to be taken away again when the market has done well. Once your money is locked in in an annuity, you can never go below that dollar amount due to the stock market.

This means you are no longer gambling on the stock market, but rather systematically playing the market with a safety net under you in case there is a fall.

Market performance is more important than advisor performance. Why? Because your advisor can't control the market, can't reliably predict the market and may at times be management fee driven not to lose your money from their assets managed column. Unfortunately, there are advisors more concerned about losing the money *they* manage and take a fee on than about losing their clients' money in general. If they lose you as a client, they could be ruined, but if they mismanage your money, your retirement could be ruined.

After training hundreds and hundreds of advisors across the country, I can honestly say I believe most of them do their best to properly manage client's money, but they can't control the market. So you must take control of the biggest threat to your money which is far and away market loss.

One of the best things an annuity can do for you besides guarantee you won't lose money and provide you with good returns, is to remove human emotion from the equation. Most money has been lost to the market because of fear and poor timing than probably any other source.

One of the most reliable sources for stock market information is Dalbar Inc. Dalbar is a quantitative analysis firm that tracks the real performance of the stock market compared to what Wall Street tells perspective customers. For 25 years they've been monitoring customer behavior on Wall Street.

As they do their analysis, year after year what they find is customers jumping ship at the wrong time and re-entering the ship at the wrong time. As they overlay data about customers with actual stock market performance, what you see is an inverse relationship. As the market goes higher, customers are sitting on the side lines because of past losses. As the market is poised to drop, you start seeing bigger and bigger participation in the market.

It's like watching an awkward dance. One partner moves left and the other partner moves the opposite direction. Human emotion takes us out of sync with the market. It comes down to selling low and buying high. For the most part we are just a few steps behind.

Dalbar properly named this "**Chasing day old bread**." By the time you hear of a good stock, it is probably already starting to peak. You've bought in just as the market is set to drop. Because of the drop and market loss, you are left on the sideline licking your wounds while the stock market is heating up again. I can't tell you how many times I hear clients say I am sitting in cash until the market shows me it is good again. By then it is too late. Stop chasing day old bread and stop letting emotions be your guide. If you don't have to worry about market loss, you can let your money ride the market up and lock in while you sleep well at night knowing the next market drop won't leave you with losses.

No annuity, even these growth focused annuities, is a get rich quick operation. Instead, they are a "don't get poor fast" protection plan that can still participate in the good side of the stock market.

9 areas of human interference

Millions of dollars of research shows that in most cases, *we* are our own worst enemy when it comes to growing our retirement money. We tend to believe ourselves to be better investors than we really are or that we've hired someone we believe will solve our problems. We don't address the issue of protect what you have first and grow it the best we can second.

There are 9 main areas which tend to trip most people up when it comes to their money. Dalbar and I will attempt to help you understand, reason and remove these areas of thinking from your financial plan.

1. **Herding.** We tend to follow a trend or crowd even in the face of an unfavorable outcome. Not knowing what to do, we follow the advice of neighbors, co-workers or TV gurus. Most tend to move with the herd after proof is shown. By then a trend may be losing its power to produce gain. Or worse ready for losses.

2. **Regret.** We tend to treat mistakes we were actively a part of more seriously than mistakes made by missing an opportunity or not reacting with proper timing. This tends to be the "chasing day old bread" idea of arriving at the end the party.

3. **Media control.** We react strongly to Media Guru's opinions without researching on our own. The media could offer a good piece of advice or a run for the hills warning. We take media personalities at their word without considering bias or human error. Are we thinking for ourselves or going with the popular trend? Warning! Some advice websites, podcasts, TV shows and articles have been found guilty of pushing advice based on who is paying for their advertising.

4. **Optimism.** This is where we believe good things will happen to us and the bad things that happen will happen to others. Yet most people aren't earning anywhere near what Wall Street professes to earn. Optimism is a good quality but can lead people to hope their way into a good return. You can't hope the market up and you can't wish it to stop when it is losing.

5. **Anchoring.** Relating our decisions to familiar experiences, even when that isn't helpful or appropriate. We try to use the world around us, our educational or career experience as background for how to make a financial decision even though we may be thinking of investing in a company, technology or brand we aren't expert in.

6. **Diversification.** This is when people try to reduce risk by spreading over multiple investments or areas of investment. Most people believe they are diversified because of many different companies or asset classes, **but most assets classes selected carry the same level of risk.** Diversification after determining downside potential serves the average investor better. Diversification can also show signs of not fully believing in an asset class so you allocate smaller amounts into the unknown.

7. **Mental accounting.** Taking on undue risk in one area and avoiding rational risk in another. For example banks have been providing less than 1% interest rates for a decade but we perceive them as low risk. To avoid low earnings we take on significantly more risk, allocating into the stock market which we know carries much higher risk. The drive for higher returns romances us to leave the realm of safety.

8. **Narrow Framing.** This is when we make decisions without considering all outcomes. As we look to get the highest return possible our thinking allows us to be overly optimistic, overlook red flags or become unbalanced in risky asset classes as we chase rates of return. 'Rate of return only' focus has led many off hazardous financial cliffs. The follow up result is going too conservative due to losses or going overly aggressive to make up for losses. Trending more aggressively only furthers the amount of pressure placed on a portfolio.

9. **Loss Aversion.** We've become desensitized to losing money. We accept it as part of being a "real investor". Many would rather risk and lose going for a big return than accept the low returns of banks. This becomes a major problem as people enter retirement age and need to count on steady income. Protecting money and understanding downside risk is imperative when creating the right growth environment plan for your money.

So much of the risk we encounter can be controlled by working with groups that have long track records of success, are familiar to the masses, have sound investment strategies in place, are heavily regulated and have a long term perspective as their horizon.

The older you get and the more times you are burned, the

question of who can I trust to protect and grow my money becomes increasingly important. **Actually it's imperative**! No one wants to scale back their lifestyle because of losses or delay their retirement because of surprise market drops.

So how does it work?

I want to tell you the tale of two Zero's. One is a very good zero and the other is a very scary zero. Right now you may be thinking, *in what world related to my money is a zero a good thing?*

When you first think of getting a zero on your money, it typically conjures up negative feelings or worry, but a zero could be the best thing for your money. Imagine for a minute that you are 65 years old and you are planning to retire in the coming year. Over the course of your career you have been a diligent saver and been fortunate for the most part with your investments.

It's September 28th, 2008 and your retirement account balance is $1 million. You've finally become a millionaire. You feel like you can finally retire and live life on your terms. No more waking up early and laughing at the boss's bad jokes. Life is great! Except on the 29th of September, the stock market drops by 777 points in a single day.

This day sparked a panic in the market and economy and the world. Within a few days major companies like Lehman Brothers were filing for bankruptcy. Companies like AIG, Goldman Sachs and all the biggest banks in the country were begging for a bail out. Your money begins to sink as the tide rolls back out to sea. The advice you are being given is to hold tight.

As you neared the bottom of the market drop, your $1 million would have dropped to $480,000. Your dream of retiring would have been pushed back a decade or more. Your advisor couldn't hold back the market or control it in any way. But it wasn't his or her fault either.

Fire moves at 19 feet per second without a break to stop it. Many watched their money be consumed like dry grass in the presence of a wild fire.

For those that had money in a guaranteed annuity, their losses were ZERO. They were contractually protected by companies that have been through this panic before. The $1 million would have remained $1 million. The power of zero saved these clients from the devastating losses suffered by the rest of us. Admittedly, I lost 38% on my 401k money. I would have killed for a zero. If you lived through this time, you know what I mean.

This same devastation happened in 2000 when the dot com bubble burst followed by the 9/11 crisis. These two events led to 3 years of back to back double digit losses. For those preparing for retirement, these market drops were devastating. For those already in retirement, it was worse. Income dried up or shriveled to the point some had to go back to work or move in with adult children.

Protecting your money with a zero might be the best safe guard available for your money. A zero that protects you against lost money and lost time is a good zero.

Where would your account values be today if you never suffered losses?

How confident would you be in your financial plan for the future if the worst you could get was a zero?

So what is a bad zero? A bad zero involves those that are using their money for income when things go negative.

Tony Robbins once said, "There's only one reason to invest. To have income in retirement."

For most baby boomers and seniors, their biggest fear isn't death, it is running out of money. Having zero income or zero money is a bad zero. Inconsistent returns, low interest rates and market loss have left many people eating into their principal. As market loss eats into your nest egg and taking money out to live on shrinks your nest egg, anticipating the zero of running out of money produces real worry.

It's imperative as you age to eliminate market loss and avoid eating into your principal by living on the money.

Financial confidence comes from your ability to produce income, not get high returns. High returns are fun to think about for a minute or brag about at a BBQ or nice evening out, but having money show up every month inspires confidence and lowers stress.

At what age are you OK with losing money? 40, 50, 60, 70?

Most people don't want to lose money at any age. However, we are fed the idea that you have to take big risks in order to get a decent return. This information comes directly from Wall Street.

If you stay safe at the bank, you lose to inflation. If you risk on Wall Street, you could lose more than you bargained for. The new low interest rate environment we live in has forced more people to take on more risk than they are comfortable with.

Having a growth focused annuity stacks the odds in your favor without having to give up the protection you seek for your money.

Imagine going to a casino every day with your retirement nest egg. As you enter you have to be honest with yourself that today you could win or break even or lose. It's the same with keeping your money in the stock market. On any given day you could win, in fact most days are winners. You could also breakeven. But there is a real chance for losses as well. Remember on September 28th almost everyone thought the market would go up forever. By the next day, their money was in real trouble.

With a growth focused annuity you can say every day, that I know today I won't lose any money and I could even have a win. Knowing you won't lose today or this year or next year or the next 10 years gives a peace of mind many would enjoy.

I'd like to share how some of these programs have performed in the past. I say past because no one can predict how these will perform in the future. We can let the past give us a picture and understanding of how a program performed without chasing day old bread. I don't have a crystal ball but I do have the past as a teacher.

Most recent 12 years repeated (non-guaranteed) hypothetical illustration table[8]

Contract year end	Mr. Example age[5]	Index return percentage[10]	Contract value	Surrender value[11]	Balanced Allocation Value[12]	Death benefit[13]	Withdrawals[14]	Cumulative annual withdrawals
At issue	-	N/A	250,000	227,500	250,000	250,000	–	–
1	70-71	6.56%	250,000	236,880	272,094	272,094	–	–
2	71-72	4.45%	250,000	255,038	286,992	286,992	–	–
3	72-73	2.60%	294,772	275,582	294,772	294,772	–	–
4	73-74	6.50%	294,772	287,449	320,575	320,575	–	–
5	74-75	5.42%	294,772	312,302	342,652	342,652	–	–
6	75-76	4.41%	360,742	347,323	360,742	360,742	–	–
7	76-77	7.99%	360,742	365,111	400,382	400,382	–	–
8	77-78	10.38%	360,742	418,337	456,519	456,519	–	–
9	78-79	0.14%	452,889	452,889	452,889	452,889	–	–
10	79-80	11.77%	452,889	482,349	528,335	528,335	–	–
11	80-81	6.53%	452,889	535,610	572,247	572,247	–	–
12	81-82	-0.57%	562,042	562,042	562,042	562,042	–	–
13	82-83	6.56%	562,042	581,642	611,713	611,713	–	–
14	83-84	4.45%	562,042	619,899	645,206	645,206	–	–
15	84-85	2.60%	662,697	662,697	662,697	662,697	–	–
16	85-86	6.50%	662,697	685,589	720,706	720,706	–	–
17	86-87	5.42%	662,697	737,546	770,340	770,340	–	–
18	87-88	4.41%	811,010	811,010	811,010	811,010	–	–
19	88-89	7.99%	811,010	846,069	900,128	900,128	–	–
20	89-90	10.38%	811,010	960,230	1,026,333	1,026,333	–	–
21	90-91	0.14%	1,018,171	1,018,171	1,018,171	1,018,171	–	–
22	91-92	11.77%	1,018,171	1,084,402	1,187,787	1,187,787	–	–
23	92-93	6.53%	1,018,171	1,204,141	1,286,508	1,286,508	–	–
24	93-94	-0.57%	1,263,566	1,263,566	1,263,566	1,263,566	–	–
25	94-95	6.56%	1,263,566	1,307,629	1,375,235	1,375,235	–	–
26	95-96	4.45%	1,263,566	1,393,639	1,450,532	1,450,532	–	–
27	96-97	2.60%	1,489,854	1,489,854	1,489,854	1,489,854	–	–
28	97-98	6.50%	1,489,854	1,541,320	1,620,269	1,620,269	–	–
29	98-99	5.42%	1,489,854	1,658,128	1,731,865	1,731,865	–	–
30	99-100	4.41%	1,823,287	1,823,287	1,823,287	1,823,287	–	–

This example shows how money might grow for a 70 year old person based on how it performed over the past 12 years. I show the past 12 years so that you can see the market going through the Great Recession and also how it climbed its way out with good years of growth.

This particular programs locks in your gains every 3 years. Once a gain has been locked in, that new number is the new baseline in the contract. Meaning that is the new protected number. If there is a drop in the market, your money will never go below your locked in amount.

If this 70 year old's money had been in this program starting in 2006, three years later her $250,000 would have grown to $294,772 and is locked in. She would have gotten the growth of 2006 and most of 2007 and avoid the major drop of 2008. $294,772 would be the new dollar amount to earn on for the coming 3 year cycle. This would also have been the lowest this account would ever be in the future except in the case of distribution or income.

The following 3 years saw growth and would have increased to $360,742 and then locked in the gain. The following 3 years saw the account value increase to $452,889. Finally you would have seen the account grow to $562,042. Then the past 12 year track record is cycled again. This particular example attempts to demonstrate 30 years of staying in a program.

Don't worry, you don't have to stay in 30 years but it's what the program shows. Most of these programs have a 5-10 year commitment.

As with all annuities, this amount could be annuitized or turned into a guaranteed stream of income the client could never outlive. However, since this is protected against losses and has a good track record for growth, we are going to manage the money ourselves so it can continue to grow. It will also allow her to pass a larger amount of money on to her heirs or in the event of higher income needs down the road, she will have more money from which to pull income. This example is the same as the previous but with her taking $12,500 each year.

Most recent 12 years repeated (non-guaranteed) hypothetical illustration table [8]

Contract year end	Mr. Example age[9]	Index return percentage[10]	Contract value	Surrender value[11]	Balanced Allocation Value[12]	Death benefit[13]	Withdrawals[14]	Cumulative annual withdrawals
At issue	-	N/A	250,000	227,500	250,000	250,000	-	-
1	70-71	6.56%	250,000	236,880	272,094	272,094	-	-
2	71-72	4.45%	238,515	243,321	273,807	273,807	12,500	12,500
3	72-73	2.60%	268,391	250,919	268,391	268,391	12,500	25,000
4	73-74	6.50%	255,891	249,534	278,290	278,290	12,500	37,500
5	74-75	5.42%	244,397	258,932	284,095	284,095	12,500	50,000
6	75-76	4.41%	285,934	275,297	285,934	285,934	12,500	62,500
7	76-77	7.99%	273,434	276,745	303,480	303,480	12,500	75,000
8	77-78	10.38%	262,171	304,029	331,778	331,778	12,500	87,500
9	78-79	0.14%	316,739	316,739	316,739	316,739	12,500	100,000
10	79-80	11.77%	304,239	324,030	354,922	354,922	12,500	112,500
11	80-81	6.53%	293,524	347,136	370,882	370,882	12,500	125,000
12	81-82	-0.57%	351,991	351,991	351,991	351,991	12,500	137,500
13	82-83	6.56%	339,491	351,329	369,494	369,494	12,500	150,000
14	83-84	4.45%	328,006	361,771	376,540	376,540	12,500	162,500
15	84-85	2.60%	373,908	373,908	373,908	373,908	12,500	175,000
16	85-86	6.50%	361,408	373,893	393,044	393,044	12,500	187,500
17	86-87	5.42%	349,914	389,436	406,752	406,752	12,500	200,000
18	87-88	4.41%	415,066	415,066	415,066	415,066	12,500	212,500
19	88-89	7.99%	402,566	419,969	446,802	446,802	12,500	225,000
20	89-90	10.38%	391,304	463,301	495,195	495,195	12,500	237,500
21	90-91	0.14%	478,856	478,856	478,856	478,856	12,500	250,000
22	91-92	11.77%	466,356	496,693	544,046	544,046	12,500	262,500
23	92-93	6.53%	455,641	538,865	575,725	575,725	12,500	275,000
24	93-94	-0.57%	553,181	553,181	553,181	553,181	12,500	287,500
25	94-95	6.56%	540,681	559,536	588,464	588,464	12,500	300,000
26	95-96	4.45%	529,196	583,672	607,499	607,499	12,500	312,500
27	96-97	2.60%	611,129	611,129	611,129	611,129	12,500	325,000
28	97-98	6.50%	598,629	619,308	651,030	651,030	12,500	337,500
29	98-99	5.42%	587,135	653,460	682,505	682,505	12,500	350,000
30	99-100	4.41%	705,378	705,378	705,378	705,378	12,500	362,500

In this example you can see the growth slows because of the stream of income but there is still growth. In fact, by year 12 she is still up by over $100,000 and she has taken out $137,500 on income to live on.

A plan that protects against losses and has a track record for consistently growing money allows you, for the most part, to live on the new money your account generates (interest earned) instead of the old money in your account (principal placed). Generating enough interest to live on comfortably removes the panic of watching your account deplete over time.

Wouldn't it be nice to have options?

You can leave your money alone and allow it to compound and grow or you can turn on income without the worry of running out of money. Having a resource to produce income means the fear of running out of money or becoming a burden on your children has been removed.

There are only two forms of income. People at work or money at work. No one wants to work forever. Not everyone can work forever. At some point your money needs to go to work for you. By producing income you get to continue working on your terms or walk away from the daily grind all together. The ability to live life on your terms is financial freedom.

One of the biggest shocks of my career has been to witness and help younger people find and get started in a program like this. Couples in their 30's, 40's and 50's that don't want to live through market drops and the stress that comes with it. Business owners that want to focus on their business or medical practice and not be a professional investor. People that have told me that going forward, they don't want to lose money ever again.

It's been very rewarding to be a part of their story.

Recently I worked with a couple that loved the idea of earning like the market, never losing again and removing the stress of watching the market. The husband tried day trading his wife's IRA after she took some losses in 2015. Admittedly, he wasn't very good at it and it was consuming a lot of his free time. However, he wasn't quite ready to commit to a 9-10 year time commitment so we found a program with a 5 year time frame.

This program follows the ups and downs the stock market for a 5 year period, but will never go below the amount of principal originally placed or after a lock in reset. The client could walk away after 5 years if he and his wife wanted or they could stay on for as long as they wanted after that.

Values

Contract Year	Client Age	Historical Annual Returns	Premiums	Withdrawals	Policy Value
At Issue	55	0.00 %	$100,000	$0	$100,250
1	55 - 56	0.00 %	$0	$0	$100,250
2	56 - 57	0.00 %	$0	$0	$100,250
3	57 - 58	0.00 %	$0	$0	$100,250
4	58 - 59	0.00 %	$0	$0	$100,250
5	59 - 60	35.99 %	$0	$0	$136,334
6	60 - 61	0.00 %	$0	$0	$136,334
7	61 - 62	0.00 %	$0	$0	$136,334
8	62 - 63	0.00 %	$0	$0	$136,334
9	63 - 64	0.00 %	$0	$0	$136,334
10	64 - 65	47.41 %	$0	$0	$200,969
11	65 - 66	0.00 %	$0	$0	$200,969
12	66 - 67	0.00 %	$0	$0	$200,969
13	67 - 68	0.00 %	$0	$0	$200,969
14	68 - 69	0.00 %	$0	$0	$200,969

The above example gave him and his wife an idea of how this program had performed. We looked at different time frames over the past 20 years, each including down years so he had a fair idea of how the program protected and could grow his money.

This example shows money growing through 2 different 5 year cycles. In the first 5 year cycle his money went through good and bad years, including 2008. After 5 years this time frame produced a 35.99% total increase which was then locked in. The $100,000 grew to $136,334. The account would never fall below the $136,334.

If he chose to go another 5 years, his $136,334 would have grown to $200,969. The total growth during this time frame was 47.41%. The new account value would then lock in place.

What's more important, getting growth on your money or eliminating market loss?

I recently asked this question to a doctor client of mine. He said getting good returns is more important than preventing loss. We discussed it and worked through the following example. What if you had $100,000 in the market going into 2008. He would have experience a 38.5% drop in account value leaving him with $61,500. Ouch! This is a rough way to get to your retirement goals.

However, the market came back like it always does. The following year the market increased by 23.5%, then 12.8%then 2011 had a flat year. His $61,500 would have increased to $75,952. Then to $86,674. By 2012 his account would be at $86,674 because of the flat 2011 performance.

His $100,000 would not come back up to $100,000 for five and a half years. Meanwhile, his annuity money would not have lost a dime and he could have participated in the market bouncing back as you can see in the examples. My doctor client said he understood the importance of eliminating market loss. It is impossible to time the market.

Most decades see eight years of plenty and two years of big drops, but the drops can take years to get back to break even. By being in a strategy that mimics the market while eliminating the losses, you pick up volatility smoothing on your money and peace of mind.

Who sleeps better, the person that loses nothing or the person that loses 20%? I know the answer and so do you. However, unless you are in the money business talking to panicked clients after a drop, you don't realize how damaging losses can be to a family, to an individual and to their physical and mental health. Just eliminating market loss could be one of the best gifts you give yourself as you march towards retirement. The next best gift will be whatever the market gives as a locked in increase.

www.yourbridgeplan.com

8. CONCLUSION

After presenting and helping people with this concept for many years, most people have one of three reactions after they read my book or work with me on this strategy. First, they either hate it completely and we never work together. Second, they wish they had heard about this incredible way of controlling and protecting their money years earlier. Third, they want to know how to get started.

There isn't much I can do for those that just plain hate the concept. Sometimes the program isn't a fit because of age, number of years someone still needs to contribute, people are single or have no kids. Other times, I meet people that like to play with their money and they are ok with the risk of Wall Street.

I have had haters come back to me later and start a plan either on themselves, a partner, spouse or a child. I find most cases people need a little more time with the idea because it is so counter to what Wall Street and traditional financial planners recommend. I recognize it requires a paradigm shift because I had to have one myself when it was first presented to me. They say it is harder to unlearn something, than to learn something new.

I can't tell you how many times I have heard, "I wish I had

learned about this concept 20 years ago." While I can't change the past, I have enjoyed helping new clients positively impact their next 20 years. Think about how much further ahead you would be if you never experienced losses. If you are just starting out, imagine growth on your money that isn't interrupted by losses or devoured by taxes.

Imagine a lifetime of being in control of your money, your financing of major purchases and the future retirement you want to have. With the whole life plan, you earn every single year. No interrupting the power of compounding interest. No sliding backwards with losses or waiting for the market to come back to break even. With the indexing strategy, you get to participate in Wall Street but a tamed version that is guaranteed not to lose. You get the benefit of down side protection without eliminating the opportunity for upside gains.

The third group that wants to learn more or see how this concept works with customized numbers based on their personal situation should work with the agent that gave them this book or reach out to our office with questions. Seeing how this works for you helps make the concept that much more powerful. Rarely is the reader the exact age as the examples in this book or has the exact amount of money as my examples. Those numbers are picked based around people I've helped and their situation. What you need is to find an agent that will patiently work with you on your situation, your numbers and your goals.

I hope this book has helped you see a different way of thinking, a different way of saving and a different way of financing major purchases. This concept helped open up a whole new world to me. My stress around growing money, losing money, paying taxes, financing cars or owning investment real estate has all changed for the better. I have total peace of mind about how I am growing my money and my client's money. And I have total peace that if something happens to one of them, that their family will be left with a large lump sum of tax-free money to help with the grieving and living out the rest of their lives comfortably. Most off all, I hope this book has given you hope for your own financial future. You deserve the future of your dreams, now go out and get it.

Request a personalized Blueprint:

Work with the author directly or one of his Bridge Plan specialists from all over the country.

Request a personalized consultation today and see how your money will grow and be protected. Contact our office today to schedule a time for us to speak. Let us show you a safer, more predictable way to achieve your financial goals.

Contact us:

Stephen@YourBridgePlan.com

888-638-0080.

To learn more about Bridge Plans and how they can help you beat inflation and earn solid returns with real assets, visit our website at:

YourBridgePlan.com

STEPHEN GARDNER

ABOUT THE AUTHOR

Stephen Gardner is a safe money specialist that lives in Salt Lake City, Utah with his wife and 3 children. He is also a national sales trainer and speaker in the financial services industry. He has often been heard saying "I am on a mission to strengthen America one family at a time." He is passionate about helping families get safer returns on their retirement funds. Although he calls himself Stephen, many of his clients and friends call him Safe Money Steve.

Stephen is also the best-selling author of A Bridge Over Troubled Wall Street and Smartest Doctor in the Room.

ACKNOWLEDGMENTS

I want to thank my wife Kacey for being my greatest supporter. Your encouragement and support have been vital to my success. You have stood by me through good times and bad. You have championed me to stretch and be the best version of myself. When the light bulb went off in my head and I finally caught the vision for how to properly use these plans, I told my wife I was quitting my job to educate people on this concept. I actually did and my wife has supported me through the whole thing. The saying that 'behind every good man is an even better woman' is most definitely true with you. Thank you.

Thank you to my children who are the reasons for my working as hard as I do. I hope to not only be a strong support for you to lean on in life, but to arm you with the necessary information that you will need to be successful in your own life.

Thank you to my parents who raised me up right and who have taught me good financial principles since I was a child. Thank you for giving me independence and support throughout my whole life. Thank you for encouraging me to be a lifelong learner and seeing me for who I would become.

Thank you, Mark Maiewski, for inspiring me. Your insight and wisdom is invaluable. Thank you, thank you, thank you!

A special thanks to Jeff Hays for all of his support over the past decade. Thank you to Julie Anderson and her wonderful parents for always loving and supporting me.

Additional Resources

Videos to help explain Bridge Plans

www.yourbridgeplan.com/videos

To work with the author or find a trusted advisor, reach out through the website to get connected.

www.yourbridgeplan.com/contact

I truly hope you enjoyed the book and found value in its message. Head on over to my website to learn more and read about more real life examples.

I have clients all over the country using this strategy to take back control of their money and their future. When done correctly it can have such a massive impact on your future. Thanks again!

Made in the USA
San Bernardino, CA
29 May 2019